THE POWER OF
PASSOVER

THE POWER OF
PASSOVER

CONTENTS

INTRODUCTION

THE FESTIVAL OF REDEMPTION

The story of the Exodus is one of the most often recounted stories in the history of the world. Since the advent of film, dozens of attempts have been made to retell the story of the Exodus, starting with the 1909 silent film *The Life of Moses* and continuing with more recent productions like *Exodus: Gods and Kings* and the documentary film *Patterns of Evidence: Exodus*. This story permeates the imagination of all who hold the Bible close in any way. And why shouldn't it? This story checks nearly every box of what it takes to be an epic story.

It begins in darkness, with a people living under the oppression of a tyrannical dictator. A man so frightened by the potential of his subjects that he forces them into hard labor. They haven't done anything wrong, but he thinks they might, and so he enslaves them. This king is so desperate to weaken this perceived threat that he turns to the outright murder of their innocent sons to feel safer in his own home. However, there is a young boy, born in secret, hidden from the powers that be, who passes through the water and into the household of the great king. Thus, a sleeper agent of sorts has been placed within the tyrannical government, ready to be activated at the appropriate time.

When this subversive agent in the house of the king is awakened, he acts swiftly and without training, resulting in a mistake. He kills an overseer of the slaves while trying to protect one of his own. His initial attempt at easing the suffering of his people falls short and he ends up running for his life from those whom he had so recently called family. As this man escapes into the wilderness, he is adopted into a new family, and the events of the past have no more sway over him.

Then one day he is called through supernatural means to finish the work that he had failed so miserably at before. Now, rather than defending a single man who was being beaten, he is called to deliver the entire nation that had been cowed under hardship and forced labor for centuries. The time for redemption had come.

This story is a story of a people moving from oppression into freedom. From sadness to joy. From darkness to light. From death to life. These are themes that are common in narratives and have been used to capture the imaginations of audiences throughout history. Specifically, this story is a reversal of fortune for the people of Israel as they are taken from the place of suffering under the hands of this totalitarian king and brought into service and relationship with the God of the universe in freedom. This story contains all of the hallmarks of a classic: water turning to blood; fire and ice falling from the sky together; plagues of frogs and lice and locusts; small fragile people walking between towering walls of water as they run from their pursuers. It features a compelling conflict, a sympathetic protagonist, and the utter annihilation of a great evil. The events leave no doubt as to who is the good guy and who is the bad guy, and in the conclusion, there is no doubt who is the victor. This story sticks in the human imagination and will not let go, and it seems as if the authors of the Bible knew this to be true.

The events of the Exodus are mentioned frequently throughout the Bible, perhaps more so than any other event. In the Torah, Israel is told to remember the Exodus as the foundation for their faith in the God who saved them out of Egypt. The Ten Commandments leverage this event several times in just a few verses.

I am the LORD your God, who brought you out of the land
of Egypt, out of the house of slavery.
—Exodus 20:2

The very opening of the Ten Commandments reminds Israel that it
was the LORD who delivered them out of Egypt and out of Slavery. In
Deuteronomy 5 we read a second account of the Ten Commandments,
and if we do a word-for-word comparison of these two passages we will
find only a few differences. The largest difference is found in the fourth
command. In Exodus, the reason that is given for Sabbath observance
is that the LORD rested on the seventh day Himself, calling us back to
Genesis 2:1-3. We are reminded of the concept of God as creator and
this idea is leveraged towards a responsive action or cessation of action
in this case. But if we turn to the giving of the Commandments in Deuteronomy 5, the text gives us a different reason for why Israel should rest
on the seventh day.

Six days you shall labor and do all your work, but the seventh
day is a Sabbath to the LORD your God. On it you shall not
do any work, you or your son or your daughter or your male
servant or your female servant, or your ox or your donkey
or any of your livestock, or the sojourner who is within your
gates, that your male servant and your female servant may
rest as well as you. You shall remember that you were a slave
in the land of Egypt, and the LORD your God brought you
out from there with a mighty hand and an outstretched arm.
Therefore the LORD your God commanded you to keep the
Sabbath day.
—Deuteronomy 5:13-15

Essentially this passage is saying, "As you were once a slave who had no respite from work, remember that you have been freed from slavery and are no longer oppressed Take the Sabbath off to rest from your labors as a reminder of this reality." Three times in the two accounts of the Ten Commandments, Israel is tasked with contemplating the reality of their redemption from Egypt by the hand of God.

Already we can see from these two short passages that there is a huge amount of focus placed on this event. And this is just the beginning. After the Book of Exodus, there are numerous other times in the Torah where Israel is reminded of how God took them out of Egypt. For example:

> For I am the LORD who brought you up out of the land of
> Egypt to be your God. You shall therefore be holy, for I am
> holy.
> —Leviticus 11:45

> But the LORD has taken you and brought you out of the iron
> furnace, out of Egypt, to be a people of his own inheritance, as
> you are this day.
> —Deuteronomy 4:20

Often this reminder is leveraged as the reason for various commands or calls for allegiance to the God of creation. Seven times Israel is reminded of their slavery in Egypt (Lev. 19:34; Deut. 10:19, 22; 15:15; 16:12; 24:22; 29:16). Three times the text reflects on the plagues and wonders that God accomplished in Egypt (Deut. 28:27, 60; 34:11). Six times Israel desires to return to Egypt or is warned against seeking to return (Num. 13:22; 14:1-3; 20:5; 21:5; Deut. 17:16; 26:68). Once, the events of the Exodus are told by someone in Israel to a person outside of

Israel (Num. 20:15-16), and four times the Exodus is told of by someone outside of Israel to others (Num. 22:5; 22:11; 23:22; 24:8).

As you can see, a large portion of the Torah after the book of Exodus speaks of the events that are recounted in just the first third of this book. These events are then used as the foundation for further ideas, commands, or warnings in the rest of the Bible. And this trend does not stop. The Exodus is brought up repeatedly throughout the remainder of the Old Testament. A reminder of what God did for Israel and to Egypt at the time of the Exodus is recounted in the books of Joshua, Judges, 1-2 Samuel, 1-2 Kings, and 1-2 Chronicles.[1] Even the books of Isaiah, Jeremiah, and Ezekiel, which were written nearly 1000 years later, speak of this story.[2] Overall, these remembrances are used in the same way as before—as an appeal to recall the reputation of the LORD, and to remember how the relationship between Him and His people began.

As we consider the events of the Exodus and the many epic scenes of power and judgment and life juxtaposed against a background of death, there is one single event that is commanded by God to be memorialized throughout history. That one event is the Passover, the 10th plague. Passover was the moment of the destruction of the first-born of man and animal within Egypt, and the means of escape from this judgment. This is the event that convinced the enemy of Israel to release his hold on the people. While not the end of the story, it does provide a central crux to the story of the Exodus. Passover is the

---

1   Joshua 2:10; 9:9; 24:5-7, 17, 32; Judges 2:1; 2:12; 6:8-9, 13; 11:13, 16; 19:30; 1 Sam 2:27; 4:8; 6:6; 8:8; 10:18; 12:6, 8; 15:2, 6; 2 Sam 7:6, 23; 1 Kings 6:1; 8:9, 16, 21, 51, 53; 9:9; 12:28; 2 Kings 17:7, 36; 19:24; 21:15; 1 Chro 17:21; 2 Chro 5:10; 6:5; 20:10; Nehemiah 9:9, 17-18.

2   Isaiah 10:24, 26; 11:16; Jer 2:6; 7:22, 25; 11:4, 7; 16:14; 23:7; 31:32; 32:20-21; 34:13; Ez 16:26; 20:5-10; 20:36; Dan 9:15; Hos 2:15; 11:1; 13:4; Amos 2:10; 3:1; 4:10; 9:7; Micah 6:4; 7:15; Haggai 2:5.

pivotal moment in time where Israel went from slaves of an oppressive regime, to free men serving a powerful and singular God. This event was accompanied by a meal—a meal that has been celebrated since the time it was first commanded. Throughout the world, even today, there are millions of people who continue to commemorate the events of the Exodus with a meal and a ceremony. But for many others who serve the God of Israel—the same God who freed Israel from Egypt—this memorial has passed out of practice. This is a significant loss in modern Christian practice, as our own Messiah fulfilled Passover in very real and meaningful ways. For the Christian, this meal and the events that surround the meal can teach us a great deal about our own faith and the God that we serve. Even more importantly, this memorial meal can teach us about our own redemption from the powers of sin and death that have held us captive. It can connect us in a way unlike any other to the God of redemption and salvation and to the one who filled up the meaning of Passover and gave it fresh life and meaning.

Let's embark on a journey together to explore the meaning of Passover for the people of God, whether you consider yourself a Christian, Jew, or something in between. Because, regardless of what you call yourself or how you practice your faith, if you are a servant of the God of Abraham, Isaac, and Jacob, Passover is for you.

PART 1
PASSOVER AND SCRIPTURE

When I was young my two older sisters enjoyed musical theater. They had me watch at least one musical production every week with them. The stories of *Oklahoma*, *West Side Story*, *Music Man*, *The Sound of Music*, and many others danced across our screen until my little mind overflowed with the words and melodies of countless songs belted out amid a narrative. One of the songs that has stayed with me over the years is from the scene in *Sound of Music* where Maria starts teaching the VonTrapp children how to sing. "Let's start at the very beginning. A very good place to start. When you read you begin with A, B, C. When you sing you begin with Do, Re, Mi." I know a lot of you now have this song stuck in your head, and you are welcome. While this song is simple and catchy, it also contains a very profound truth. When starting to study a subject for the very first time, it is important to begin with the fundamentals. It does not matter how well you think you can accomplish the task before you, or how well you seem to know the subject matter. If you have never engaged the topic in any serious way before, then start at the beginning and ensure you know the fundamentals before moving on to more difficult disciplines within that subject. As you learn you will begin to discard bad habits and misconceptions and become firmly grounded in the fundamentals of the discipline you have chosen.

When it comes to a subject like the Bible, the first order of business for any true student is to read the Bible. Read it several times. Become familiar with the feel of the various stories, authors, and books of the Bible, because they each have a different flavor and focus. Even when a book seems to be telling the same story, such as much of the books of

Kings and Chronicles, there is a different overall theme being explored in each account, so familiarize yourself with them. Then when you begin to examine a specific topic in the Bible you should begin with the introduction of that topic, once again firmly grounding yourself in the fundamentals of that one topic.

When we get to the topic of Passover, Exodus 12 would seem to be a reasonable place to start. This chapter contains the initial commands surrounding the first Passover as well as the narrative and commands for memorializing the event. However, before delving into the text of this chapter, we need to discuss something even more fundamental to the concept of Passover: the definition of the Hebrew word *Pesach* (פסח, pronounced peh'-sakh), translated as "Passover."

Pesach

The word *Pesach* is found throughout the Hebrew Bible, and in every instance, it is referring to the events of Exodus 12 or the memorial sacrifice and meal that accompany this event. So examining this word alone is not particularly helpful. But this word is derived from a root word that is used in seven other places in the Hebrew Bible. The root of the word *Pesach* can provide insight into the concepts that it encompasses. The root of *Pesach* is *pasach*, and in Hebrew, it is spelled exactly the same as *Pesach* with the only difference being a single vowel point. So, while we find this word in seven places throughout the Hebrew Bible, we don't have to go far to begin our search. Three of the occurrences of *pasach* are in Exodus 12 (Exodus 12:13, 23, 27). In all three of these verses, the word is translated as "pass" or "pass over." But one of these verses uses a completely different Hebrew word that means "pass over," revealing that there is a nuance to the word pasach that implies more than simply that of walking by or floating past.

For the LORD will *pass through* [avar (עָבַר)] to strike the
Egyptians, and when he sees the blood on the lintel and the
two doorposts, the LORD will *pass over* [pasach (פֶּסַח)] the
door and will not allow the destroyer to enter your houses to
strike you.

—Exodus 12:23

In the English translation of this verse, the issue can be hard to
spot as translators have done their best to ease any confusion. But in
Hebrew, the potential issue becomes a bit clearer. In Hebrew, the first
word in this verse is the word *avar* (עָבַר). This word is a verb that
literally means to "pass over, or by, or through."[1] More concretely this
word means to transition from one place to another. The beginning
of this verse says the LORD will "Pass through (עָבַר, *avar*)" Egypt to
strike them, but then later in the same verse, the LORD will "Pass
over (פֶּסַח; *pasach*)" the houses with blood on the doorposts. Do you
see the problem? If *pasach* simply means to "pass over," then there is
no difference at all between *avar* and *pasach*. Now in truth, there is no
problem. The word *pasach* does indeed contain the definition of "pass
over" within the range of meaning for the word, but the nuance of the
word is different than the word *avar*. And in this nuance, we can gain
a better understanding of just what it is that the LORD did for those
who covered the doorposts of their house with the blood of the lamb.
To get a better handle on this, let's look at the other four instances of
the word *pasach* in the Hebrew Scriptures and see if we can catch a
glimpse of this nuance in action.

---

1 Brown, Driver, Briggs and Gesenius. "Hebrew Lexicon entry for `abar". "The NAS Old
   Testament Hebrew Lexicon".

The first occurrence of this word after Exodus 12 is found in 2 Samuel 4:4. I will highlight the words that are used to translate *pasach* in the upcoming verses for ease of reference.

> Jonathan, the son of Saul, had a son who was crippled in his feet. He was five years old when the news about Saul and Jonathan came from Jezreel, and his nurse took him up and fled, and as she fled in her haste, he fell and became **lame**. And his name was Mephibosheth.
> —2 Samuel 4:4

In this first example, the son of Jonathan became lame after falling from the arms of his nurse as a child. The words "and he became lame" are the translation of the word *vayepaseach*: *Va* (and) *ye* (he) *paseach* (became lame). In this verse the word *pasach* means lame. This indicates that Mephibosheth suffered a permanent injury, which might have been severe enough to require him to be carried for the rest of his life. But as we will see later, it more likely caused him to walk with a limp.

The second two occurrences of this word are both found in 1 Kings 18:

> And Elijah came near to all the people and said, "How long will you go **limping** between two different opinions? If the LORD is God, follow him; but if Baal, then follow him." And the people did not answer him a word.
> —1 Kings 18:21

> And they took the bull that was given them, and they prepared it and called upon the name of Baal from morning until noon,

saying, "O Baal, answer us!" But there was no voice, and no
one answered. And they **limped** around the altar that they had
made.
—1 Kings 18:26

Again, we find in these two verses where the word *pasach* is translated as limping. How is this word related to Passover? Did God limp
past the houses of the Israelites when He saw the blood on their doorposts? That doesn't hold true with what we know of the LORD and His
power, so we must go further. Well, there is one last verse to examine.
Perhaps this verse can give us that extra bit of nuance to help us understand this word better.

Like birds hovering, so the LORD of hosts will protect Jerusalem; he will protect and deliver it; he will spare and rescue it.
—Isaiah 31:5

Growing up in a farming community you didn't have to go far to
find a person who had chickens. We had some ourselves for a time.
Anyone who has ever had chickens who have been allowed to hatch
chicks would probably recognize what this verse is describing. When a
mother hen feels that the lives of her chicks are threatened, the chicks
will run under the wings of their mother. The mother will then fluff out
her wings and begin to hop back and forth on her feet like a boxer. This
action is a protective and defensive action meant to make the mother
look bigger so that the predator will hopefully back away and leave
them alone. This defensive posture also places the life of the mother in
danger while protecting the lives of her young.

When we examine all four of these verses in conjunction with
the three instances of this word in Exodus 12, we can see that the

word *pasach* describes a back and forth movement. 1 Kings 18:21 highlights this: "How long will you limp between two opinions?" The NIV and other translations render this, "how long will waver between two opinions?" This description suggests that a person's foundation is unsteady because they are constantly shifting and unsettled rather than being firmly grounded. This word seems to describe a movement that can look like a limp, or like a fighter preparing to defend himself or another. We see this simile of the LORD likened to a mother bird used in other places in Scripture as well, only in these cases it is without the use of the word *pasach*. One example of this is:

> Like an eagle that stirs up its nest, that flutters over its young, spreading out its wings, catching them, bearing them on its pinions.
> —Deuteronomy 32:11

The mother bird in the passage is described as fluttering over her young, protecting them and training them by bearing the young on pinions into the sky. And so, when we encounter the word Passover or *Pesach*, we should also consider the nuance that this word contains. This is the action that God took towards Israel in Exodus 12:23, and this action is not God simply looking at the door and moving on as so many movies attempt to depict this event. Rather, it is as the verse states: "the LORD will *pasach* His people and He will not allow the destroyer to enter in." He will act as protector to His people by standing guard over them, and in so doing He will keep death from their doors when the destroyer comes. This is not a passive flight over the house or a casual stroll without stopping. It is not a limping action or a cloud of green smoke simply passing by. This verb, *pasach*, is active and describes the LORD standing at the door of the house as a guard or bouncer, turning death away from the inhabitants of that home. And so with this, let's now return to Exodus 12 and begin our examination of Passover in full.

The First Passover

There are two things to initially consider when digging into the topic of Passover for the first time. There is the first Passover—that is, the events of the book of Exodus and what they can tell us about the God that we serve. Then there is the Passover Memorial that was initiated and was then to be kept yearly after this first Passover. Exodus 12 discusses both and it does so in an interesting way. Rather than simply listing everything required for the first Passover and then moving on to what is required for the Passover memorial, the text bounces back and forth (or perhaps limps?) between both in a manner called parallelism. Parallelism is when a text will state one thing and then repeat that same thing in another way. The parallel structure of this passage is laid out in the following way:

Exodus 12:1-13 – Instructions for first Passover

Exodus 12:14-20 – Instructions for Memorial

Exodus 12:21-23 – Instructions for First Passover

Exodus 12:24-27 – Instructions for Memorial

Exodus 12:28-42 – The Narrative of the First Passover

Exodus 12:43-51 – Instructions for Memorial

The text moves between what was to occur, or what did occur at the first Passover, and instructions for how to conduct the Memorial in later years. Let's examine each of the elements and actions involved in the first Passover, discussing their significance in this unique event. Afterwards, we will discuss the memorial aspect of Passover.

The Lamb

For the first Passover, the ritual began five days before the meal. On the tenth day of the month of Aviv, the month known as Nisan today, every family was to select a lamb without blemish from their flocks and bring it into their home and live with it. In our western minds, we think of a tiny perfectly white lamb, cute and cuddly and adorable. But that is not what is described. The lamb was to be a year old. A "lamb" of this age would be nearly full grown. It would be capable of reproducing, it would have horns, and it would be rather large. This was not the baby sheep we often imagine. Add to this that the lamb being without blemish does not mean that it had no spots or coloring. This meant that the lamb was not lame, injured, or deformed in any way. Any whole and healthy specimen would suffice for this sacrifice.

One part of the wholeness of this sacrifice was to last throughout the entire process. In Exodus 12:46 we discover that the lamb was not to have any of its bones broken. No bone was to be broken at any point during the life, slaughter, or consumption of this lamb. This makes a simple sort of sense. An animal that had survived a broken bone would be considered imperfect and thus not qualify for Passover. But no broken bone during the slaughter and eating of the lamb? What could possibly be the reason for this? That was one of the mysteries of this command. And yet, John, in his gospel, employs this enigmatic command concerning the Passover lamb to emphasize Jesus' role as our Passover sacrifice.

Additionally, the lamb was not required to be a sheep. Indeed, in English, the word lamb inherently means a young sheep, but that is not the case in Hebrew. As we see in Exodus 12:5, this lamb could be taken from the sheep or the goats. The lamb was then to be kept separate from the rest of the flock and brought into the family home for the days that passed between the 10th and the evening of the 14th of the month. Then on the 14th of the month, the lamb was to be slaughtered by each family in the community and its blood was to be applied to the doorposts of the house.

The Blood and the Altar

The act of painting the doorpost of your house in blood is something that can be a bit hard to stomach. Many of us in the modern West simply cannot stand the sight of blood. We live in a sterile world where blood is not part of our daily experience. This was not the case in the ancient world. In the ANE (Ancient Near East), blood was a very common thing to encounter, especially to those whose livelihood involved animals in some way. Animal sacrifice and animal slaughter was a regular occurrence. Nobody ate meat without slaughtering an animal, and that often meant killing it yourself. In the same way, worship of many of the gods involved sacrifices of various sorts and blood was the means of worship. The type of sacrifice that is described in Exodus 12 was not an uncommon form of sacrifice.

In verses 21-22, we read some details about how this particular sacrifice was to be accomplished that clue us into the nature of the sacrifice. The animal was to be slaughtered and the blood was to be collected in a basin. Once this had occurred, a branch of hyssop was to be dipped in the blood and used as the brush to paint the door frame and mantle. Interestingly, this basin was not just any bowl or jar that was used to collect the blood. Rather the basin was a feature of the threshold of the home. In ancient Egypt and throughout much of the ancient world, the threshold of a home also served as an altar of worship. The Hebrew word translated as basin, *saf* (סף), in verse 22 is also translated as "threshold," "door," or "door-post," elsewhere in the Bible. The book, *The Threshold Covenant: Or the Beginning of Religious Rites* by H. Clay Trumbull records that it was common in the ancient world for the threshold to contain a basin for catching the blood of a sacrifice.[2] This location of the threshold of a house served as an altar to the god that the house was dedicated to. You see, the ancient world was full of gods that people could choose to worship. Monotheism as we conceptualize it today was a foreign concept to ancient peoples. Nearly everyone was polytheistic and recognized multiple gods. Every culture had gods that would oversee every level of human life and inter-action, from national to individual. The gods that were worshiped the closest to the individual would be the god of the house, which would be chosen by the elders of the house and then worshiped for gener-ations within that household. It was a common practice to sacrifice at the threshold of the house as an appeal to the god of the house for any number of reasons including protection, fortune, wealth, health, fertility, and more. In *The Threshold Covenant*, Mr. Trumbull states that the Passover sacrifice mimics a dedication sacrifice common in surrounding cultures. He then spends a full 20 pages exploring the connection of Passover to a threshold sacrifice and the implications of such an understanding.[3]

---

2   H. Clay Trumbull, *The Threshold Covenant: Or the Beginning of Religious Rites* (New York: Charles Scribner's Sons, 1896), 206-207.

3   Ibid., 203-222.

Once the blood was collected in the basin at the threshold of the home, it was then to be spread to the doorposts and mantle using a branch of hyssop. This blood would outline a portal on all sides of the door to the house, not just the top and sides. This is an action that would have created a distinct marking that would separate Israel from Egypt, regardless of where a person lived in the land. Additionally, this sacrifice also served as a means of dedicating every household in the community to the LORD. It was a declaration of allegiance to the God of their forefathers. But commanding the sacrifice in this way teaches us something extremely important about God. When God came to Israel to deliver them from the oppression of the enemy, He met Israel where they were in their worship practices. At the beginning of His relationship with Israel, the LORD allowed them to sacrifice the first *Pesach* lamb in a way that was familiar to them. It was only later at Mt. Sinai once a covenant had been cut between God and Israel that He began to change their worship practices to teach Israel about who He is. The tabernacle as the place of worship is not established until chapter 25 of Exodus. And it is Leviticus that describes the new ways of worship. In this, we discover a bit of the character of the LORD. God meets people where they are when they first enter into a relationship with Him. It is only at a later point that He starts to expect more of us.

The Menu

The menu for the first Passover was a bit limited. The lamb was to be roasted over a fire and not boiled with water. When it was roasted they were not to remove the head or feet from the lamb. This is stated alongside the later instructions in verse 46 that no bones were to be broken in the preparation of the Passover lamb. The menu was then rounded out with some unleavened bread and bitter herbs as side dishes.

Now, there is no consensus as to what the bitter herbs would have constituted. In modern Passover meals, horseradish is often used, but lettuce, parsley, or celery are also considered to be valid options for the bitter herbs as well. Regardless of the specifics, the bitter herbs serve as a physical reminder of the bitterness that Israel lived under while in Egypt. It is a tangible taste of the slavery and oppression that were so pervasive for Isreal that it took their very sons from them. This reminder is a central feature of the Passover memorial meal. The place where you came from was bitter. Don't forget.

And yet Israel forgets. By chapter 14, Israel is already complaining about being brought out of Egypt. And beginning in Numbers 11, we start to read of a general sense of longing toward Egypt among the Israelites. They view the past in Egypt as being better and long for the food they ate there.

> Now the rabble that was among them had a strong craving.
> And the people of Israel also wept again and said, "Oh that we
> had meat to eat! We remember the fish we ate in Egypt that
> cost nothing, the cucumbers, the melons, the leeks, the onions,
> and the garlic. But now our strength is dried up, and there is
> nothing at all but this manna to look at.
> —Numbers 11:4-6

Israel looked back on Egypt and they remembered the food that they had to eat there. No mention of the hardship and slavery and death. "At least we had cucumbers..." And this is human nature. We go through a rough time on the way to something better and we look back at the past with rose-colored glasses. The past seems better because I didn't have to worry about the current problem I am facing. But the lesson of the bitter herbs for Passover is to remind us that the past is not better. Our lives before our redemption were not good. Those days were times of bitter hardship that kept us from truly growing.

The matzah, or unleavened bread, is also to be a central part of Passover—and not just for Passover but for the week that follows as well. For seven days no leavened bread was to be eaten by anyone in Israel. In verses 34 and 39 we read during the narrative of this night that the reason for this was that the people left in such a hurry that they were not able to wait for their bread to rise. Thus, they kept their dough in kneading bowls and carried it with them. The symbol of matzah is very deep and powerful, but I will focus on this symbol later in this book.

The Manner of Eating

The night of Passover the people were to eat as though they were expecting to leave at any moment because they were. They were to keep their sandals on their feet and eat with their staff in their hands. The first Passover was not a leisurely event. It was something that was done in haste because no one knew the exact timing of when they would need to leave.

The urgency that is described is meaningful as it speaks to us of our own redemption. The moment of redemption is not a leisurely affair. It is something that is not to be delayed or drug out. We are to engage in that moment with gusto and zeal, knowing that our redemption is at hand.

Additionally, the Passover lamb was not to remain until morning. Anything that was not eaten during the night was to be completely destroyed with fire. Now, this is something that is a common practice in sacrifice. The burnt sacrifice of Leviticus 1 was to be completely burned up immediately. Nothing was eaten of it at all. However, in the case of other sacrifices described in Leviticus, some parts of the sacrifice were consumed by the priests and worshippers, but any remaining portion of the sacrifice had to be disposed of after a certain number of days. Out of all of these other sacrifices, though, there is one other that was to be destroyed the next day.

> And the flesh of the sacrifice of his peace offerings for thanksgiving shall be eaten on the day of his offering. He shall not leave any of it until the morning.
> —Leviticus 7:15

The sacrifice of thanksgiving was one where the worshiper would bring an animal to the tabernacle, slaughter the animal, and take the suet from the kidneys and liver and offer them on the altar. The priests in general who were serving in the tabernacle on that day would receive the breast of the animal and the priest who offered the sacrifice received the right thigh. The worshiper then received the remainder of the meat of the animal back to share with family and friends. The purpose of this sacrifice was to give the person an opportunity to express gratitude and celebrate by hosting a party and inviting their loved ones and God to participate. In the case of the thanksgiving sacrifice, the party only lasted one night. In the morning, anything that was left of the sacrifice was destroyed by fire.

So the question is, how are these two experiences, Passover and the thanksgiving sacrifice, similar? Both are communal events of testimony and praise. In the thanksgiving sacrifice and subsequent party, the worshiper would share with everyone who was part of the meal the reason for the party. A testimony of the faithfulness of God would be declared and His name would be lifted up and glorified as all would engage in praise from a heart of gratitude. Likewise, the Passover meal is a form of thanksgiving sacrifice. God was freeing Israel from the oppression of Egypt. He heard their cries at the end of Exodus 2, and He was responding to those cries to deliver. In that moment of deliverance, there was to be a sense of gratitude toward God for what He was in the process of doing. And in the memorial meals that followed in subsequent years and centuries, this meal and sacrifice were to be approached in the same way: with praise and thanksgiving, lifting high the name of God in gratitude for the redemption that He purchased on our behalf.

The Firstborn

This particular aspect of Passover has been a source of discomfort for many people. It can be challenging to reconcile a loving God with destructive acts such as this, the flood, or the many other judgments that we read of throughout the Bible, up to and including Revelation. Why was it necessary to destroy all of the firstborn of Egypt? While the answer to this question may not be clearly spelled out, we can connect some dots in Scripture to gain a better understanding. The key to this understanding is found in this chapter.

> For I will pass through the land of Egypt that night, and I
> will strike all the firstborn in the land of Egypt, both man and
> beast; and on all the gods of Egypt I will execute judgments: I
> am the LORD.
> —Exodus 12:12

This verse raises a question: how is striking all the firstborn of man and beast a judgment against the gods of Egypt? To understand the answer to this question, it is necessary to study ancient Mesopotamian culture. It is my belief that in the ANE, the firstborn sons of a family were those who were expected to fulfill the role of priests for the various gods for the family. This idea is hinted at in several different passages in the Bible, including Genesis 2, Exodus 13 and 19, Numbers 3 and 8, and Isaiah 61.

In Genesis 2, Adam was given two tasks that he was to accomplish in the garden:

> The LORD God took the man and put him in the garden of
> Eden to **work** it and **keep** it.
> —Genesis 2:15

In Hebrew, the words used for working and keeping the garden are the words *avad* (עְבַד) which means to "work, serve, minister, or worship,"[4] and *shamar* (שָׁמַר) which means to "guard or keep safe."[5] Now there is nothing inherently special about these words in their usage here other than their proximity to each other. Every other time in the Bible when we find these two words used in conjunction to describe the duties of a person, they are describing the duties of a priest or Levite:

> They shall keep **guard** (*shamar*) over him and over the whole
> congregation before the tent of meeting, as they **minister**
> (*avad*) at the tabernacle. They shall **guard** (*shamar*) all the fur-
> nishings of the tent of meeting, and keep **guard** (*shamar*) over
> the people of Israel as they **minister** (*avad*) at the tabernacle.
> —Numbers 3:7-8

---

4   Brown, Driver, Briggs and Gesenius. "Hebrew Lexicon entry for `abad". The NAS Old Testament Hebrew Lexicon.

5   Brown, Driver, Briggs and Gesenius. "Hebrew Lexicon entry for Shamar." "The NAS Old Testament Hebrew Lexicon."

And this is just one example. We find these two words used in conjunction in several other places throughout the Hebrew Bible as well (e.g., Num. 8:25-26, 18:5-6; 1 Chron. 23:32; Ezek. 44:14). In every case, it is the priests and Levites who were to perform this action of guarding and serving. From this, we can catch our first glimpse of the role that Adam was to play in the garden. This firstborn of men was to serve as a priest in the Garden of Eden. And this practice continued through the ages and became the cultural norm in early Mesopotamian cultures.

Although it may initially seem like a stretch to suggest that the firstborn were expected to serve as priests, when we look at Exodus 13 and Numbers 3, we find additional evidence that supports this idea:

> Consecrate to me all the firstborn. Whatever is the first to
> open the womb among the people of Israel, both of man and
> of beast, is mine.
> —Exodus 13:2

This command on its own does not have to mean that the firstborn were set apart as priests, but when we compare this passage to Exodus 29:1 and Leviticus 8:30, we find that the priests were specifically consecrated and set apart from the rest of Israel for the purpose of serving the LORD in the tabernacle.

In Exodus 19, at the base of Mt. Sinai, before the giving of the Ten Commandments, and long before the Golden calf or the appointing of the tribe of Levi to the office of priest, Israel had priests:

> Also let the priests who come near to the LORD consecrate
> themselves, lest the LORD break out against them...And the
> LORD said to him, "Go down, and come up bringing Aaron

with you. But do not let the priests and the people break
through to come up to the LORD, lest he break out against
them."
—Exodus 19:22, 24

Who were these priests at this time if not the Levites? Well if we
look forward to the book of Numbers we just might discover who filled
this role.

And the LORD said to Moses, "List all the firstborn males
of the people of Israel, from a month old and upward, taking
the number of their names. And you shall take the Levites for
me—I am the LORD—**instead of all the firstborn among
the people of Israel**, and the cattle of the Levites instead of all
the firstborn among the cattle of the people of Israel."
—Numbers 3:40-41

For all the firstborn among the people of Israel are mine, both
of man and of beast. On the day that I struck down all the
firstborn in the land of Egypt I consecrated them for myself,
and **I have taken the Levites instead of all the firstborn
among the people of Israel**.
—Numbers 8:17-18

The command to list the firstborn and have them pay their redemption price, which we first see in Exodus 13 alongside the command to
consecrate the firstborn, is then shifted in Numbers 3. What transpires
in Numbers seems to be a trade of those who would serve God in
His holy place. Rather than the firstborn entering into service to the
LORD, it is the Levites that are to take up this role. Although it is not

explicitly stated in the Bible that the firstborn served as priests before the events described in these passages, we can infer this based on the multiple biblical hints that suggest such an arrangement.

In Isaiah 61, we read something interesting in relation to the role of priest—not priests of the past, but priests of the future:

> Strangers shall stand and tend your flocks; foreigners shall be your plowmen and vinedressers; but you shall be called **the priests of the LORD**; they shall speak of you as the ministers of our God; you shall eat the wealth of the nations, and in their glory you shall boast. Instead of your shame there shall be a **double portion**; instead of dishonor they shall rejoice in their lot; therefore in their land they shall possess a **double portion**; they shall have everlasting joy.
> —Isaiah 61:5-7

Throughout the Torah and the Bible as a whole, it was understood that the firstborn of a family received a double helping of the father's inheritance. If the father had three sons, his property was split four ways and the first born received two portions. If the father had eight sons, then the inheritance was split nine ways, and again, the firstborn would receive double the inheritance of the other brothers. Significantly, in Isaiah, when the prophet speaks of Israel, he calls them priests and promises that they will receive a "double portion." And in Exodus 4:22, when Moses is told to go and stand before Pharaoh and request that Israel be set free to worship, Moses was to call Israel "God's firstborn," a title that carries over into the prophets.

Unfortunately, this is just an inference that we can make based on the information provided in these passages and other related passages. But it is not directly stated in the Bible. This state of firstborn priests is not clearly stated in the Bible, and it is not attested to in the historical record that I have been able to find. Regardless, the pieces seem to fit extremely well. And so with this in mind, when God tells Moses that this destruction of the firstborn was to be a judgment against the gods of Egypt, we can see how this might be. If the firstborn served as priests, then the temple system of Egypt would have been destroyed completely. Thus, when the LORD then says that all firstborn are His, we can infer that this was the beginning of turning Israel away from the worship practices of Egypt to teach them how to worship Him alone. No longer were the firstborn to be priests to whatever household god the family served or to be trained to serve in the temples of other gods. Now they were to be dedicated to the LORD and serve Him alone. For Egypt and Pharaoh, the destruction of the temple system would have highlighted the power of the LORD over the gods of Egypt. Their worship hierarchy would have been completely destroyed as the priests of their gods all fell to this final plague. This plague also served as repayment of sorts on Egypt for their destruction of the sons of Israel. We read in Deuteronomy 32 and elsewhere that vengeance and repayment belong to the LORD, and this plague is an example of that principle in action.

Death of the Firstborn

On the night of the Passover, it was the firstborn of all men and beasts that were at risk. The destroyer was going to move through Egypt and there was no stopping it. The only thing that could be done was to declare allegiance to the God of creation by putting the blood of the Passover lamb on the doorpost of one's house, and in doing so, all of the firstborn in the household were protected from the destroyer as he moved through the land.

When we turn to the New Testament and the death of Jesus, we find this theme being revisited once again. This time, instead of the firstborn of the nations being subject to the destroyer, it is Jesus, the firstborn of creation, who allowed Himself to become the victim of the destroyer. By being the firstborn who fell under the judgment of the destroyer, Jesus became the means by which all men can gain protection from the destroyer in the future.

Between the Evenings

In Exodus 12:6 we read that the Passover lambs were to be slaughtered at twilight of the fourteenth day of the month, and this is repeated in Leviticus 23. This seems pretty self-explanatory, except this is not what the Hebrew says. The Hebrew does not say at twilight. Rather, it is read literally as "between the two evenings." What does this mean to offer between the evenings?

We find this phrase used elsewhere in the Torah, and perhaps by examining these other places we can discover how ancient Israel interpreted this phrase. Fortunately, we don't have to go far to discover another time when this phrase is used:

> Now this is what you shall offer on the altar: two lambs a
> year old day by day regularly. One lamb you shall offer in the
> morning, and the other lamb you shall offer at **twilight**. And
> with the first lamb a tenth measure of fine flour mingled with
> a fourth of a hin of beaten oil, and a fourth of a hin of wine
> for a drink offering. The other lamb you shall offer at **twilight**,
> and shall offer with it a grain offering and its drink offering,
> as in the morning, for a pleasing aroma, a food offering to the
> LORD.
> —Exodus 29:38-41

This passage tells us of the daily sacrifices that were to occur in the tabernacle and temple, one in the morning and the other "between the two evenings." Fortunately for us, we have records of when the evening sacrifice occurred in the temple. Jewish historian Alfred Edersheim records that the afternoon sacrifice would be slain around 2:30 in the afternoon and would be offered on the altar around 3 PM.[6] From this we can determine that the phrase "between the evenings" does not mean at twilight but rather is an idiom for any time after the sun begins to descend in the sky until it sets and a new day begins. This might seem like simply a bit of trivia, but I promise that it will come in handy later.

Gold and Silver

Before leaving Egypt, Israel stopped by the homes of the inhabitants of Egypt and asked them for goods of gold, silver, and clothing. These were three of the most valuable items in the ancient world. It is a bit baffling to consider that Egypt freely gave them these items after the absolute destruction that had happened to the economic stability of their homeland. We would assume that the Egyptians would have held on to this wealth knowing that they would need wealth in the upcoming days. But when we look at how this action was described in the text, we find that it is described as Israel plundering Egypt.

In warfare, plundering is the typical action of a victorious army after the defeat of their enemies. And in Exodus 13:17-18, the manner of Israel's leaving is also described as an army. And yet, Israel was led into the wilderness to avoid armed conflict. So while Israel is described as plundering Egypt and is described as an army marching in forma-

---

6   Alfred Edersheim, *The Temple: Its Ministry and Services as They Were at the Time of Jesus Christ* (New York: Flemning H. Revell, 1908), 144.

tion, the means of that plunder was a peaceful request after God had fought their battle. It is as if Egypt, in their grief and despair at the great losses that they had just suffered, did not want to take the chance of angering Israel's God further by not complying. They had failed to comply with this God more than ten times and had suffered an ultimate and humiliating defeat after defeat. So, out of fear of further retribution, they simply gave the Israelites what they asked for.

This action has also been explained as Egypt attempting to bribe Israel to leave. The Egyptians wanted the Israelites gone, so they offered them whatever remaining goods they had, fulfilling the very request that the Israelites had made in chapter 5.

Regardless of the motivation of Egypt while they were handing over their wealth, there is more to this plunder than simply the victors taking the spoils from the defeated. In this action, we learn a bit about God's justice system. Just as the judgment on the firstborn was repayment in kind on Egypt for their destruction of the sons of Israel, this act of plundering Egypt was also repayment in kind. It was a means of gathering back wages for people who had been treated as slaves. For centuries Israel had worked without payment, slaving away for the good of Egypt. Their lifeblood was spent benefiting and enriching Egypt, and so now the lifeblood of Egypt is spent enriching Israel. We see this again when God commands that slaves who are set free in the seventh year are to be sent away with enough to make a new start for themselves (Deuteronomy 15:13-14). This is God's system of justice, which ensures that Israel receives financial reward as they leave the land of their unpaid labor.

Mixed Multitude

I often try to imagine what it would have been like to be a person living in ancient Egypt during the plagues described in the Bible. At what point would I be forced to consider that my way of life and national identity was faulty? How many of the plagues would it have taken for me to recognize that the way that we were treating these foreigners in our midst was evil? I am fortunate to have examples from history to look back on and see that this way of interacting with those around us is wicked. I can look back on not just the events in Exodus, but the practice of slavery in America, the Soviet gulags, the Armenian genocide, the Jewish Holocaust in Nazi Germany, and many other travesties of the last few centuries. I can see the evil in all these things. But what would it take if I did not have these pertinent examples of the past to look back on? What would it take for me to change my belief that it was acceptable to mistreat those that I saw to be different or dangerous?

Well, in Exodus 12:28, we read that a "mixed multitude" left Egypt alongside Israel. There were a multitude of people in Egypt who recognized the fault in their actions, and rather than remain in Egypt when the time came to escape, they went along. In doing so, these multitudes aligned themselves with Israel and their God. These people would have been traders and merchants and travelers from all over the world, as well as Egyptian nationals who no longer agreed with or aligned with the Egyptian government. Later in verse 48, we catch sight that this mixed multitude was to be incorporated into the people of Israel. The stranger who sojourns with Israel, the *ger* (גֵּר), can participate in the Passover memorial, but only after they have joined themselves to the people of Israel through the rite of circumcision.

In the Septuagint, the second-century BCE Greek translation of the Hebrew Scriptures, this word *ger* is translated as "proselyte" (προσελθη). A proselyte is a person who had converted to the Hebrew religion and forsaken their former foreign identity. But if we consider this fully, we may find that proselyte is not, perhaps, the best way to understand this word.

Why do I say this? Because in Exodus 12:38 we read that only after a *ger* was circumcised could they join in Passover. This seems to imply that there would have been *gerim* who lived among Israel who had not officially joined Israel as full converts through circumcision. So *ger* is perhaps not best understood as a full convert or proselyte. Rather, the *ger* can be best understood as a friendly foreigner who lives among Israel and worships their God, but does not have the inheritance rights that the native-born would have had. This type of person could be circumcised or not. They served the same God and were friendly to Israel, even if they never took on the label of Israel.

Regardless, the fact that there was a multitude of people who were not blood descendants of Abraham who left Egypt alongside Israel demonstrates that the redemption from Egypt was open to anyone who decided to sacrifice the lamb and apply the blood to their doorposts. Anyone who dedicated their household to the LORD was separated from Egypt, or the citizenship of their homeland, and was welcomed to join Israel.

430 Years

One of the final statements made in the narrative of Passover is that this event happened 430 years to the day since Israel had come to Egypt. 430 years is a long time, but it is this passage of time that connects the text back to Genesis 15 and the covenant that God made with Abraham:

> Then the LORD said to Abram, "Know for certain that your offspring will be sojourners in a land that is not theirs and will be servants there, and they will be afflicted for **four hundred**

years. But I will bring judgment on the nation that they serve, and afterward, they shall come out with great possessions.

Now there may seem to be a contradiction going on in the text here, but that is not the case. These two passages start their year count from different points. But that is not what I wish to highlight here. Rather, we can see from the connection of these two passages that Passover was not simply a great event of freedom for Israel. It was also the fulfillment of a covenant promise that the LORD made with Abraham more than 400 years before. In Genesis 15, it was the LORD, or at least symbols that represent Him, that was the one that walked between the pieces. In doing this, God is taking all of the responsibility for ensuring the terms of the covenant upon Himself.

And what are the terms of the covenant? God would redeem Israel from slavery and provide nationhood for the children of Israel. This would then be followed by an occupation of the land of Canaan. So when we get to Exodus 12, we find that it is Passover that finally accomplishes this promise. Passover demonstrated God's character trait of faithfulness to Israel for this new generation, which is something that the nation as a whole needed to experience. This character trait is best captured by the word chesed (חסד), which we will examine in more depth shortly.

Whether 400 or 430 years, no one can deny that the Passover was promised to Abraham and was then carried out in Egypt. God made a covenant in which He promised that He would bring about the desired outcome, and He ensured that this outcome occurred.

As we can see when we compile all of these items together, the event of the first Passover was much grander than even the most epic of movies could hope to capture on film. The judgment on the gods of Egypt as their priestly system was wiped out; the dedication to the

LORD that was declared by each person who slaughtered the lamb and displayed the blood on their doorpost; the back payments that were plundered from Egypt by the armies of Israel who never lifted a sword; the inclusion of a multitude from the nations who joined Israel alongside the native-born; the fulfillment of a promise that had been made centuries before. If we don't take the time to study the culture and context of the story, we may not fully understand all of these events and their significance. It is this deeper understanding that can help us to better appreciate the full scope of just what God was accomplishing, not just for Israel, but also for the whole world. Never before in the history of the world has a nation been created from within another nation without a rebellion or civil war. The creation of Israel was solely the result of God's will.

The elements of Passover provide a wealth of insight into the depth of action that God took to save Israel from Egypt. In what He commanded to be accomplished, God began to shift the Israelites' hearts away from the ways of the culture that surrounded them. But the elements take us much further than what happened 3500 years ago. It is in these elements that we begin to catch glimpses of the greater Passover that occurred in the death and resurrection of Jesus. They teach us about the redemption that His blood provides as a way to enter into a relationship and covenant with the LORD. This is a topic that we will explore in greater detail in an upcoming chapter.

The Passover Memorial

We discovered in our reading of Exodus 12 that the text does something odd. It does not simply tell us of the first Passover. Interspersed throughout this chapter, alongside the instructions and narrative of the Passover, are a series of commands for Passover to be memorialized in later generations. Three times in this one chapter we read of the future memorial event that is to be held yearly in remembrance of what the LORD did for Israel on that day. Then, as we continue forward in the Torah, there are at least six more times that we read commands related to this future observance of Passover in Israel. This memorialization was to be a time to remember the hardship that Israel suffered under and the freedom and escape from death that was found in the blood of the sacrificial lamb. But as we explore what the Bible has to say about this memorial meal, we discover that the future events are not a one-to-one recreation of the first. Some modifications were to be accomplished in the memorial that were not part of the original event. There are also some items from the original that are missing from the memorial. For now, we will focus solely on what the Bible has to say about the Passover memorial. The Festival of matzah will be discussed separately in a later section. For now, let's dive into the text regarding the Passover memorial and all that it entails.

In Exodus 12:14, we read that this day shall be a memorial for Israel. It is to be a time for remembrance of the events of the past. The word translated as memorial in this verse and elsewhere is the word *zicrone* (זכרון). This word finds its root in the word for remember, *zacar* (זכר). In English, when we hear the word remember, we connect the idea of remembering to the process of having thoughts about our past. Remember simply means to have an event of the past that we focus on in our minds for a time. We experience this when we have a moment of silence to memorialize an event. Simply sit quietly for a moment and reflect internally on that past event. But if you wish to think about football or work, you can do that too, because no one is policing your thoughts. In English, there is no action necessary when something is remembered. The thought is enough.

Hebrew does not work in the same way. Hebrew is an action-oriented language, and so when we read words that appear passive to us in English, we should stop and consider the action that is implied. For example, the word *shema* (שמע) is often translated as "hear." To our English minds, this means simply allowing sound waves to bounce off of your eardrum. We can even extend the idea of attaching a mental recognition and acknowledgment of that sound. But once again, there is no action necessary when having heard something. But the word *shema* does not work that way. *Shema* also means to obey. A person who has heard, according to the Hebrew understanding, does not simply allow sound into their ear. Rather they accomplish some action with what has been heard. Likewise, in Hebrew thought, a man does not know how to build a house until he has accomplished it with his own hands. Simply watching YouTube and having the process in his head is not to know a thing. Knowing a thing is to be actively engaged in the thing.

When we consider the word *zacar* ("remember"), we need to recognize that there is always an assumed action connected to the thoughts of the past. It means to recall the past and then to act in the present based on what was remembered. So then, in Exodus 2:24, when it says that God remembered His covenant with Abraham, it does not mean that he had previously forgotten as if this covenant had somehow slipped His mind. Rather, it means that God had not, until this point, taken any action to accomplish the terms of the covenant that had been made previously, but now the time had come. Now He was ready to act.

A memorial, a *zicrone*, is then an item or action that has been instituted to cause a person to recall the events of the past, which should then impel the person towards some sort of action. Exodus 12 is the first time that we encounter this word in Scripture. It just so happens that this particular *zicrone* is itself an action that is to be taken. There is a sacrifice, a meal, and a seven-day festival all acting together as part of this memorial. When we read verses 14-20, the primary focus of the memorial is the festival of matzah or Unleavened Bread. This festival begins on the 15th of the month and continues for seven days. There is little recounted in Exodus 12 that applies to the Passover memorial specifically, but let's go through the few items in this chapter that do.

In Every Generation

In verses 24-27, we discover that this rite that was to be kept forever was to be a teaching moment for the next generation. The future sacrifices, the future meals, this memorialization of this event was to point younger generations back to the events of that first night. But it is even deeper, as Deuteronomy 24:18 seems to imply that every person in Israel, in every future generation, was to view themselves as having been brought out of Egypt personally. Remember, Israel at the time of Deuteronomy was the second generation that had been brought out of Egypt. The only individuals who had come out of Egypt at Passover would have been children at the time of their escape, and yet Deuteronomy states that "you were a slave in Egypt." Deuteronomy 10:19 likewise says that "you were strangers (*ger*) in the land of Egypt." Not only is Passover and the matzah memorial to be kept perpetually, but each person who participates in this memorial is also to see themselves as having been present for the first Passover.

Each one of us who is alive today is to see ourselves as having gone through the night of watches. *You* were a slave in Egypt. *You* cried out to God for freedom. *You* sacrificed the lamb and applied the blood to your doorposts. *You* waited in anticipation of the destroyer. *You* passed through the waters and were delivered into freedom. Passover is not just a historical event with no relevance to us in the modern world. The meal that we participate in is to be a time to reflect on these events of the past as we eat a meal similar to the one that was shared by those who were there.

And for the Christian, viewing ourselves as having been part of the original Passover should not be much of a stretch. We were all slaves to sin and death. We have all been redeemed from death. We have all eaten of the lamb that turns back the destroyer, and we have all passed through the waters of death into life. Our story, our conversion story, is a story of Passover for every one of us. And the Passover memorial is the perfect time to reflect on these events in our personal history.

The Sign of Circumcision

In Exodus 12:43-51, we find that Passover was an exclusive event. There was a process that had to occur before a person could celebrate even the memorialization of this event. A person had to take on the sign of circumcision, the sign of being joined in covenant to the family of Abraham before they could engage in the Passover memorial sacrifice and meal. Now, the exclusion of non-covenant members does not apply to the celebration of the festival of matzah. We read in Exodus 13:7 that there is to be no leavening found in the borders of Israel during this week-long festival. But for Passover, circumcision was required. Why? To understand the significance of circumcision, we need to go back to Genesis and examine the initial command for circumcision. There, we will get to the root of what is being required of the *ger*, or stranger, in this passage.

In Genesis 12, God called Abraham to leave the house of his father and to travel to "the land that I will show you," and Abraham did just that. He took his beautiful wife, packed up his belongings, and traveled from Haran in Aram to the land of Canaan. Attached to this initial blessing was a promise that God would make of Abraham "a great nation." But there was a problem with this promise from Abraham's point of view. Sarah was barren. She had always been barren. We were told of her barrenness in Genesis 11. But Abraham trusted God and pressed on in faith and did what was asked of him, believing that God was capable of fulfilling His promise. Skip forward several years to Genesis 15, and once again we find God speaking to Abraham about His promise. It seems as if this came in a moment of great doubt about whether God would actually hold up His end of the bargain.

> After these things, the word of the LORD came to Abram
> in a vision: "Fear not, Abram, I am your shield; your reward
> shall be very great." But Abram said, "O Lord GOD, what
> will you give me, for I continue childless, and the heir of my
> house is Eliezer of Damascus?" And Abram said, "Behold, you
> have given me no offspring, and a member of my household
> will be my heir." And behold, the word of the LORD came
> to him: "This man shall not be your heir; your very own son
> shall be your heir." And he brought him outside and said,
> "Look toward heaven, and number the stars, if you are able to
> number them." Then he said to him, "So shall your offspring
> be." And he believed the LORD, and he counted it to him as
> righteousness.
> —Genesis 15:1-6

Abraham was promised a great reward once again, but Abraham was beset by doubts. "I continue childless, and the heir of my house is Eliezer of Damascus." Abraham seems to be saying, "God, you haven't solved the problem yet, and I am having trouble seeing you in this." Abraham is having a crisis of faith. Can he trust this God whom he had chosen to follow? Was this a trustworthy God? There were plenty of gods in the cultures that surrounded them, and none of them were trustworthy. The gods were fickle. Was this God fickle too? But into this moment of doubt God simply speaks, "Your very own son shall be your heir" and as the "number of the stars...so shall your offspring be." This statement by God was once again taken as truth by Abraham, and his trust that the LORD would fulfill His promises was counted as righteousness to Abraham's account. But then more years pass and still nothing. Still no sign that his wife is going to bear a child, and so Sarah and Abraham conspire to accomplish God's will through human power.

Enter Hagar, the Egyptian slave that Sarah possibly acquired when they spent time in Egypt near the end of Genesis 12. You see, it was a common practice in the ANE for a barren woman to choose another woman to act as a surrogate mother to a child for her husband. Since artificial insemination and in vitro fertilization were not possible for several millennia, the way that this was accomplished was for the husband to sleep with the surrogate until pregnancy occurred. The child that was born of this union was legally the child of the father and of his wife. For a woman of means such as Sarah, a servant was a viable and culturally acceptable option to act as a surrogate in her place. And so Sarah offers up Hagar to be a surrogate to produce an heir for Abraham.

This attempt to accomplish God's will through human power did produce a child, but in the end, it ultimately failed. God's promise was not fulfilled through this. Ishmael was not the heir that God had intended for Abraham. But it seems as if God does not disabuse Abraham of his idea that Ishmael was his heir until Genesis 17. When we reach this chapter, 13 years have passed with Ishmael, the son of Hagar and Abraham, serving in the position of the heir of the family name and line of Abraham. As the chapter opens, God comes to Abraham, and once again he reiterates the terms of the covenant from chapter 15. It has only been two chapters for the reader, but 13 years for Abraham and Sarah.

> Behold, my covenant is with you, and you shall be the father
> of a multitude of nations. No longer shall your name be called
> Abram, but your name shall be Abraham, for I have made
> you the father of a multitude of nations. I will make you
> exceedingly fruitful, and I will make you into nations, and
> kings shall come from you. And I will establish my covenant
> between me and you and your offspring after you throughout
> their generations for an everlasting covenant, to be God to
> you and to your offspring after you.
> —Genesis 17:4-7

Once again there is a promise that Abraham will have children and that those children will become a multitude of nations. The implication here at the beginning of the chapter is that Ishmael is not the one, and this idea is solidified by the end of the chapter. Instead, there is another. The child of the covenant is yet to come, and so the covenant is reiterated and is then sealed with a sign:

> This is my covenant, which you shall keep, between me and
> you and your offspring after you: Every male among you shall
> be circumcised. You shall be circumcised in the flesh of your
> foreskins, and it shall be a sign of the covenant between me
> and you.
> —Genesis 17:10-11

Contrary to some teachings, circumcision is itself not a covenant. Rather, circumcision was to be the sign of those who have entered into the household of Abraham. It is a sign or a symbol of the covenant that God had cut with Abraham. The symbolism contained in this act is profound and speaks directly to the distinction of peoples that is to be made in Exodus 12. Are you part of the covenant of nations or not? The answer to this question will determine whether you can participate in the Passover memorial sacrifice and meal.

As we continue in Genesis 17, we read near the end of God's speech in verses 15-16 the last major miracle that is to occur in the fulfillment of this covenant. Sarah is to be the mother of this child. The barren woman was to become the mother of nations. The impossible will come to pass and the promise of the covenant from so many years before will begin to be fulfilled.

If we step back and examine circumcision as a whole, we discover that circumcision is a sign as Genesis says. It is more than a simple act of cutting away skin. Think about it. Circumcision is a physical act that demonstrates that the promises of God are not accomplished through human means or according to human understanding. Abraham physically cut off part of his body that was used for fathering children, and yet Abraham became the father of nations according to the promise only after taking this action. Likewise, Sarah, who had been barren her entire life and who was well beyond childbearing age, was to become the mother of nations according to the promise. Contained in the symbol of circumcision is a demonstration that this promise of God was to be accomplished through no human ability. And yet, when we combine these two situations, cutting off the foreskin and barrenness, we get a full revelation that the child that was to be conceived was conceived by supernatural means. There was to be no thought in the minds of anyone that it was the power of Abraham that brought forth this child in his old age, or that Sarah was simply a very late bloomer. It was not the power, authority, or ability of Abraham or of Sarah that fulfilled the promise of God. It was the faithfulness of God to His promises alone that accomplished this miracle.

So when we turn to Passover, we find the same thing occurring in this story. Israel is pictured as an army, and yet not a single person lifted a sword to accomplish their freedom. We see Israel in a place of powerlessness and the promise seeming beyond their grasp, and yet they are granted freedom. Egypt was too strong and Israel had been slaves too long and had become weak. We see this not only in Passover but also in the crossing of the Red Sea:

> And Moses said to the people, "Fear not, **stand firm, and
> see the salvation of the LORD**, which he will work for you
> today. For the Egyptians whom you see today, you shall never
> see again.
> —Exodus 14:13

The redemption and fulfillment of the promise that God had made so many centuries before, to deliver Israel and make a nation of them, was accomplished entirely by the power of God. No human power could accomplish this redemption. This is what the sign of circumcision demonstrates. "Not by might, nor by power, but by my Spirit," says God through the sign of circumcision. So while those who were native-born in Israel were circumcised on the eighth day and brought up with this symbol of the power of God in their flesh, any gentile that wished to participate in the Passover Memorial rites had to take on this same mark of submission to the will of God. Their participation in the circumcision was an act of faith that the God of Israel would remain faithful to His promise and that they wanted to be included in that promise.

So while Paul is correct that circumcision is not required to be saved, there is a circumcision that remains in effect even today. Not a circumcision of the flesh, but a circumcision of the heart. Once again, we find a symbol which describes a person putting themselves second and allowing God to have His way in their lives. For those who apply the blood of the Passover Lamb of Jesus, it is a circumcision of the heart that is required to participate in Passover. It speaks of an attitude of humility before God by placing oneself second to God and His kingdom. It is a tacit agreement to allow Him to take charge in your life and to allow His power to accomplish His promises.

Other Passover Commands

If we move out of Exodus 12 and continue through the Torah, we find more commands that are associated with Passover. Exodus 35:22 states that the Passover memorial sacrifice is not to remain until morning just like at the first Passover. Deuteronomy 16 makes it clear that the Passover memorial sacrifice is not to be done at a person's home but rather is to be sacrificed in the "Place that the LORD will choose to make His name dwell." This chapter of Deuteronomy 16 also uses an odd word choice to describe how the lamb is to be prepared. Additionally, throughout the Torah, this festival and two others are given a unique name: *chag* ("festival"). This is a unique type of festival that requires something of the worshiper. Finally, Numbers 9 states that some were not able to keep the festival as described, and so a "second Passover" was instituted. Let's go through each of these items and discover what more we can learn of this event, and along the way, let's solve some potential issues.

Second Passover

In the second year of Israel's travels through the wilderness, while they were still camped at Mt. Sinai, the LORD comes to Moses to remind him that it is time to keep the Passover memorial. This comes just days after the Tabernacle had finished construction and was dedicated. But while Israel was preparing for their observance of Passover, an issue came up.

During this year at Mt. Sinai, the people had learned that a person who was unclean because of touching a dead body as described in Numbers 17 was not to eat of the Passover sacrifice. And as the second year approached, there were men in Israel who recognized that they were unclean and that they could not participate in the Passover meal for this reason. What were they to do? Were they to eat of the sacrifice while unclean, or were they to not participate in Passover? And so Moses goes before God and presents Him with this problem.

The solution to this problem is the institution of the second Passover. One month after Passover, those who were unable to participate in the original celebration due to reasons such as uncleanliness or travel were allowed to come together and observe the holiday in the same manner as it was celebrated in the previous month. This would presumably also apply to any other legitimate excuses for not participating in the original celebration. No one who wanted to take part in Passover was to be forbidden due to matters beyond their control.

Numbers 9 is also the only place where we discover that the Passover Memorial, both the first-month and second-month observances, was to feature the bitter herbs as part of the menu. We also find that the Passover memorial was to be kept "according to all its statutes and its rules." But which statutes and rules are these? They were not to put the blood on their doorposts anymore. Are there other commands that were given as part of the first Passover that were not to be included in subsequent Passovers? What is the distinction between the commands and statutes for the memorial of Passover and the commands that were given only for the original Passover? The Torah is not clear. And so we can do only the best we can with the information that we have to honor this special day.

Boiled or Roasted?

Speaking of doing our best to interpret the text, there is one turn of phrase that has caused some consternation among scholars regarding how the memorial Passover was to be cooked.

> Do not eat any of it raw or **boiled** in water, but roasted, its head with its legs and its inner parts.
> —Exodus 12:9

In Exodus 12, the command for the preparation of the Passover lamb was that the lamb was not to be boiled in water. The issue arises with the word translated as boiled (*bashel* [בשל]). When we turn to Deuteronomy 16 and read the same instructions we see the issue:

> And you shall **cook** it and eat it at the place that the LORD your God will choose. And in the morning you shall turn and go to your tents.
> —Deuteronomy 16:7

Here in Deuteronomy 16, the word translated as "cook" is the same word that was used for boiled in Exodus 12, *bashel*. What is going on here? Some have suggested that this is evidence of different authors or different editors for the Torah, or that Moses simply had a "senior moment" and wrote the wrong thing. Another option is that this is a change from the instructions from the first Passover. Moses recognized that the subsequent Passover celebrations were not the original and so there was a change in how the lamb was to be prepared in recognition of this fact. Add to this that we do know from Exodus 29:31 and 1 Samuel 2:13 and elsewhere that this was how the animals that were sacrificed were cooked on the tabernacle premises. In both cases, the sacrifice in question was to be boiled (*bashel*) as part of the preparation of the sacrifice for eating. So perhaps it was expected that the Passover sacrifice was to be cooked in the manner of other sacrifices.

The problem with this line of reasoning is that there seems to be a conflict in the text that needs to be solved. The solution to this conundrum is that the word *bashel* is not reserved for boiling. It is used in a whole slew of different ways throughout the Bible:

> So Tamar went to her brother Amnon's house, where he was lying down. And she took dough and kneaded it and made cakes in his sight and **baked** the cakes.
> —2 Samuel 13:8

In this verse, we find that Tamar applied the action of *bashel* to the cakes that she was preparing for Amnon. Did she boil them? Was this some sort of proto-bagel? The simple answer is that she simply baked the cakes in the hearth. We find another instance of the word *bashel* being used in various ways in the book of 2 Chronicles. In this case, the verse is speaking of how the Passover lamb was prepared, so this is extremely pertinent to this discussion:

> And they **roasted** the Passover lamb with fire according to the rule; and they boiled the holy offerings in pots, in cauldrons,

and in pans, and carried them quickly to all the laypeople.
—2 Chronicles 35:13

In this passage, both the words "roasted" and "boiled" are the word *bashel*. You see, the word *bashel* does not inherently mean to boil. This word is applied to vineyards that are ripe in Joel 3:14 and Genesis 40:10, and it is translated as "baked" in Numbers 11:8 to describe what Israel did to the manna they gathered. When we look throughout Scripture and combine the various usages of this word, we discover that it describes any kind of bubbling action that is observed during cooking.

When you bake bread, such as Tamar did in 2 Samuel, air forms inside the bread and can seem as if it is boiling. Bubbles will form and pop, albeit much more slowly than water. When you look over ripe fields of grapes, the vines appear as though they are bubbling out of the plant, and when you roast meat over an open flame, juices boil forth out of the meat. Each of these visuals is described by the word *bashel*, and so we should not assume that it means only to boil.

So when we read in Exodus 12:9 that the meat should not be *bashel*, we must not miss the following words: "in water." This modification of the word *bashel* defines exactly what kind of *bashel* is being accomplished with the lamb. The lamb was to be roasted over a fire as Exodus 12 states and as 2 Chronicle 35 confirms. Any attempt to introduce a conflict into the Torah based on the usage of this word is misplaced.

Chag

There is one final difference between the first Passover and the Passover memorial that should be discussed, and that difference is found in where the celebration was to occur. The first Passover was one in which the people sacrificed the animal in their home and then left the next day to head towards the mountain where they were to meet God. But in the memorial, the people were to leave their homes and travel to the place where God chose to make His name to dwell, as we read in Deuteronomy 16. We find in this a corollary of action in both instances. The trip taken in both cases consists of leaving one's home and going to the place of God's choosing. We find a difference, however, in where and when in this timeline that the lamb was to be sacrificed. And just where is the place where God chose to make His name dwell? We will look at this in the upcoming section. As we read through the Torah of the commands concerning Passover, we find three other festivals that are to be treated the same way, with a trip from the house to the place of God's name.

> Three times in the year you shall keep a feast to me. You shall keep the Feast of Unleavened Bread. As I commanded you, you shall eat unleavened bread for seven days at the appointed time in the month of Abib, for in it you came out of Egypt. None shall appear before me empty-handed. You shall keep the Feast of Harvest, of the first-fruits of your labor, of what you sow in the field. You shall keep the Feast of Ingathering at the end of the year when you gather in from the field the fruit of your labor. Three times in the year shall all your males appear before the Lord GOD.
> —Exodus 23:14-17

The three festivals that required this bit of travel were Passover (or matzah depending on the verse), Shavu'ot (Pentecost), and Sukkot (Tabernacles). Out of the seven festivals listed in Leviticus 23, it was at these three times a year that the men were to drop everything to worship and celebrate. As we read about the festivals, we discover that these three were not known by the traditional word for holiday, *moed* (מועד). Rather, these three festivals have a unique name applied to them: *chag* (חג), a word that means pilgrimage festival. Each of these festivals required the men of Israel to make a pilgrimage to the place of God's Name. If we compare the timing of these festivals we discover that they occurred just after a harvest of some sort. It was during these times that the first-fruits of the various harvests were to be brought before the LORD as a tithe or tribute.

> When you come into the land that the LORD your God
> is giving you for an inheritance and have taken possession
> of it and live in it, you shall take some of the first of all the
> fruit of the ground, which you harvest from your land that
> the LORD your God is giving you, and you shall put it in
> a basket, and you shall go to the place that the LORD your
> God will choose, to make his name to dwell there.
> —Deuteronomy 26:1-2

The timing of the *chag* celebrations during the harvest seasons— barley for Passover, wheat for Pentecost, and the fall produce for Sukkot—made it easy for the offering to be transported to the taber- nacle or temple before it could spoil. But it was more than that. The *chag* celebrations were a time of community that brought all of Israel together to honor and worship the LORD. They were always more than simply a history lesson or time of celebration. These festivals were full-fledged lessons in the theology of the LORD, and they continue to be so today.

The Place Where God's Name Dwells

In Deuteronomy 16, we read that the Passover lamb was to be sacrificed in the place where God chose to place His name, but this is not the first time that we read of this particular idea. The first time that we read of a place where the LORD will choose for His name to dwell is in Exodus 20, just after the giving of the Ten Commandments:

> An altar of earth you shall make for me and sacrifice on it
> your burnt offerings and your peace offerings, your sheep
> and your oxen. In every place where I cause my name to be
> remembered, I will come to you and bless you.
> —Exodus 20:24

But where is the specific place where God will cause His name to be remembered? Now, many will tell you that this place is the location of the tabernacle or the temple based on passages such as Deuteronomy 12:5. When we compare the two passages of Exodus 20 and Deuteronomy 12 the temple or tabernacle seems like a good fit. These are the places where the altar is to be built. These are the places where sacrifices are to be offered. But then we get to Deuteronomy 16 and this idea begins to break apart:

> You may not offer the Passover sacrifice within any of your
> towns that the LORD your God is giving you, but at the
> place that the LORD your God will choose, to make his
> name dwell in it, there you shall offer the Passover sacrifice, in
> the evening at sunset, at the time you came out of Egypt. And
> you shall cook it and eat it at the place that the LORD your

God will choose. And in the morning you shall turn and go
to your tents.
—Deuteronomy 16:5-7

You will offer the sacrifice in the place that God will choose to
make His name dwell. Compared to Exodus 20 and Deuteronomy
12, so far so good. But consider verse 7: "And you will cook it and eat
it in the place that the LORD your God will choose." Uh-oh. There
is not a single person out there that would suggest that the Passover
lambs for every person in Israel were to be cooked and eaten in the
temple. So where exactly is the place where God chooses to make His
name dwell if it is not the place of worship?

Well, if we track this language throughout the Bible we find that
the place God chose for His name is clearly spelled out in several
places throughout Scripture. We read of this place when Solomon
dedicates the temple in 2 Chronicles 6:6, 1 Kings 11:32, 14:21, 2
Kings 23:27, Nehemiah 1:9, among others.

But I have chosen Jerusalem that my name may be there, and
I have chosen David to be over my people Israel.
—1 Chronicles 6:6

The place where God chose to make His name dwell is not the
temple itself, but rather the city in which the temple is located. This
place is Jerusalem. Now, this might seem like it is just a bit of trivia,
but as we will discover in chapter two, there was a lot of disagreement
in ancient Judaism over where exactly the Passover was to be sacrificed, and it is these verses and passages that play a huge role in the
confusion.

The Festival of Matzah

Following Passover, or rather overlapping Passover, there is another festival. We have already encountered this festival because Passover cannot be mentioned without also mentioning the festival of matzah or the Feast of Unleavened Bread, which is fist mentioned in Exodus 12:15-20. From here on, this festival will simply be referred to as matzah with a capital M. This festival is a seven-day observance in which Israel eats no leavened bread for seven days. That is all that we are told about this particular holiday; only that there is an expected change in diet. We first encounter this festival in Exodus 12 alongside the commands for and narration of the first Passover and the interspersed instructions for the later Passover observances. But why is this festival so important? What can this week-long change of diet teach us? Exodus 12 provides an early understanding of what this festival commemorates:

> So the people took their dough before it was leavened, their kneading bowls being bound up in their cloaks on their shoulders.
> —Exodus 12:34

Israel's quick departure from Egypt meant that they had to take their dough with them before it had a chance to rise, resulting in unleavened bread. This is the first hint of the reason for this festival. We read about this festival again in Exodus 13:3-11. In this passage, it is stated that this service is kept because "of what the LORD did for me when I came up out of Egypt." Once again, the idea of a memorial is present in the text. This festival serves as a reminder of the events of Passover for a week following the meal. Truly, Passover was a significant event in the course of history if an entire week-long celebration was commanded as part of a yearly memorial event.

Practical Matzah

In the modern world, this can be a bit hard to understand. What is so difficult or time-consuming that a person could not leaven their bread before leaving? Why not let it rise while on the move for that matter? My wife makes two loaves of bread a week and she can leaven a loaf of bread in around an hour or two! Why was Israel unable to have leavened bread on their way out of Egypt? Why wait days to leaven their bread? When I first began to contemplate the meaning behind this festival, these questions seemed so vital. I realized that there must be something I was missing, and upon further investigation, I learned that the explanation involves scientific knowledge and modern technology. The fact is that our modern method of leavening and how it occurs in most situations, as well as our knowledge of chemical and biological substances that can induce leavening, are at the root of these questions. Our modern disposition can distract us from what the Bible is trying to teach through this festival.

Secondary to this, what does leaven symbolize or signify? If leavened products were to be removed from the borders of Israel, and this is a shadow picture that is meant to teach something, there must be more going on than simply a spring cleaning. The commands surrounding this festival are limited to *chametz* (leaven). There is no indication that dust was to be removed or laundry was to be done or floors swept, only that leavened products were to be removed. To answer these questions, we will have to look even more into the way that bread was made in the ancient world and then we should look to the ways that leaven is used as a symbol by other Biblical authors.

So why was it so difficult to leaven bread in the ancient world? The simple fact is that there were no yeast packets in the ancient world. Yeast is a bacterium, a concept that would have meant nothing to a person that lived before the invention of the microscope. Not a single person from the ancient world would have thought that there were microscopic organisms that lived in the world and that it was their waste gas that was responsible for the bubbles that formed in bread dough. The results of the interactions of bacteria or germs or any other microorganism would not be attributed to these causes. Rather these interactions were ascribed to the unknowable at best or some sort of magic at worst. Because of this, there was no quick or simple way to leaven bread. Instead, the dough had to be allowed to rest, and while resting it would gather yeast from the air around it. The process used in the ancient world would be something similar to making sourdough bread today.

For anyone who is not familiar with this process, it begins with only flour and water. All you need to do is mix and wait. Then mix and wait. Then mix and wait. This process is repeated daily and with each mixing, the dough is fed with more flour and water. After about five to six days, the dough will have collected enough yeast from the environment to be used as a starter for making loaves of bread. Now, all that a person has to do once they have a starter is to mix a portion of the starter into a new lump of dough made from flour and water and allow the dough to rest for around twelve hours. In this time, the yeast that is in the starter will work its way into the remainder of the loaf, and you will have a fully leavened loaf.

When you understand the basic process of making leavened bread in the ancient world and recognize that this was the only way to produce it, it becomes clear that the command to observe a seven-day festival of unleavened bread is more than just a prohibition on consuming or making leavened bread. Through implication, a person in the ancient world would by necessity need to discard their starter each year and then begin the process fresh after the Festival of Unleavened Bread had passed.

Now, this might seem like a good idea to many who are unfamiliar with the process. Start over with your starter dough each year? Of course! It is easy to see that every time that you make bread from a starter in this way that some of the original flour that was put in from the very beginning would be part of every loaf. But if you were to read forums of those who regularly engage in making sourdough, you will discover that the longer a batch of starter has been around, the better it is thought to be. Simply search sourdough starters on the internet and you can find some that are up to 235 years old that are readily available for purchase. Every loaf of bread from that starter would have some 235-year-old flour in it.

So when Israel was told to not eat anything leavened, there is more going on here than simply a limiting of their diets. Rather, the entire process of bread making was interrupted for the year. The starter that seemed reliable and had been used faithfully for an entire year had to be discarded. After the festival, everyone would need to start over from scratch making their bread so that it could be leavened; a process that took most of a week. But there must be more to this holiday than simply a restart of the bread-making process in Israel. There must be deeper themes underlying this holiday, which can be explored by examining what the Bible says about it in other places, and specifically by considering the symbolism of leavening as it appears in the Bible.

To start, let's continue reading the Torah to see if we can find any additional information that might provide insight into the symbolism of leavened and unleavened things. The first place we will look is Exodus 13. Here we find something quite profound when we can connect the dots of the different topics of this chapter. When we open chapter 13 we read of the consecration of the firstborn of man and animal in verse 2, and then the text shifts to the Festival of Unleavened Bread for the next 8 verses. Then in verse 11, the text turns back to the topic of consecrating the firstborn and the process of how to accomplish this act.

Why does the chapter begin and end with a discussion of consecrating or sanctifying and redeeming the firstborn of humans and animals? Why is it that between these commands on firstborn are the commands for the Festival of matzah? Let's see if we can find other locations in the text where these two ideas are put side by side. We don't have to turn far to find another occurrence:

> You shall keep the Feast of Unleavened Bread. Seven days
> you shall eat unleavened bread, as I commanded you, at the
> time appointed in the month Abib, for in the month Abib
> you came out from Egypt. All that open the womb are mine,
> all your male livestock, the firstborn of cow and sheep. The
> firstborn of a donkey you shall redeem with a lamb, or if you
> will not redeem it you shall break its neck. All the firstborn of
> your sons you shall redeem. And none shall appear before me
> empty-handed.
> —Exodus 34:18-20

Again we find these two ideas: the Festival of Matzah and the redemption of the firstborn juxtaposed in the text. Is there something deeper at play here? Well, let's consider what we have learned already. The sanctification of the firstborn of Israel and destruction of the firstborn of Egypt demonstrated a new way of worship. The God of Israel displaced the gods of the nations through this action and revealed

Himself as the one and only true God who is worthy of worship. The firstborn of Israel became the new priests in the worship of the LORD until they were replaced by the sons of Aaron and the Levites in Leviticus 8 and Numbers.

Let's also consider the practical outcome of the Festival of Matzah alongside this. That is, throwing out the old starter dough and doing without leavened bread for a week and then starting all over with a new batch for the coming year. When we consider both of these points of data and their implications, we find that there is a theme of starting over or beginning anew. These two items work together to demonstrate a fresh start to the way that things have been done before. And when we find the meaning of the symbol of leaven, we can discover just what kind of fresh start Israel was expected to engage in during this memorial celebration.

To understand how the concept of starting fresh can be applied in the contemporary world, we need to consider the symbolism of leaven in scripture.

The Symbol of Leaven

The symbolic significance of leaven can be a bit difficult to pin down. This symbol is used in different ways throughout the Bible, and at times it can seem contradictory. For example, during the Festival of Unleavened Bread, there is to be no leavened product found in Israel. The bread that was offered alongside the majority of sacrifices on the altar was to be accompanied by unleavened bread (Lev. 2, 6-7). The consecration ceremony of the priests was to feature unleavened bread as well (Exod. 29; Lev. 8). On the other hand, during the Festival of Shavu'ot (Pentecost), it was leavened bread that was to be featured as part of the celebration (Lev. 23:17), and there was a leavened loaf that was to be included alongside the unleavened loaves of a thanksgiving sacrifice (Lev. 7:13). So while matzah, ordination, and most sacrifices feature only unleavened bread, Shavu'ot and thanksgiving sacrifices both featured leavened bread. So is it a positive or negative symbol?

Add to this that when Jesus uses leavening as a symbol in the Gospels, He uses this same symbol in both a positive and a negative manner as well:

> He told them another parable. "The kingdom of heaven is like leaven that a woman took and hid in three measures of flour, till it was all leavened."
> —Matthew 13:33

> How is it that you fail to understand that I did not speak about bread? Beware of the leaven of the Pharisees and Sadducees." Then they understood that he did not tell them to beware of the leaven of bread, but of the teaching of the Pharisees and Sadducees.
> —Matthew 16:11-12

In Matthew 13, leaven is positive and the kingdom of heaven is likened to the leavening of bread. But then in chapter 16, it is the leavening of the Pharisees and Sadducees that Jesus warns His disciples against. Which is it? One seems to be positive and another seems to be negative. How can this single symbol be used to demonstrate both? Unless leaven is just that—a symbol—and there is something that connects both the positive and the negative to each other. If we continue to Matthew 16:12, we are told what leavening is in both parables:

His warning: the teachings of the Pharisees and Sadducees, who were proud and saw themselves as the arbiters of truth and righteousness, should be avoided.

Throughout the New Testament, this symbol of leavening is used, but its use is not limited to a single thing. Leaven is not pride. Leaven is not teaching. Leaven is not simply evil or malice. Rather, leaven is used as a symbol to describe anything that can be introduced to a person or community that can then begin to permeate, infect, or spread through the whole. The teaching of the kingdom of heaven can spread in a person or community until it has fully penetrated the whole, winning a great victory for the Kingdom. By the same token, so can evil, malice, arrogance, pride, or destructive doctrine. Each of these specific items is represented by the symbol of leaven and used to indicate attitudes that will tear down a person or community. Just as leavening can be either forbidden or accepted as part of a celebration or sacrifice depending on the context, so too leavening can be used as a symbol of either good or evil. The point of the symbol of leaven is that it can be anything that spreads from one person to the next until an entire community is saturated.

That brings us back to the Festival of Matzah, this seven-day memorial of Israel's escape from Egypt. Contained in this festival is the idea of starting over or beginning fresh. If we consider this week alongside the events of Passover, we see that this is a consistent theme of the holiday. The old oppressor is driven out, and now a fresh beginning is initiated in the lives of those who have been freed. But there is also the idea of participating in self-affliction by eating the bread of affliction—not as an act of flagellation but as an act of humility and of putting away one's puffed-up pride and arrogance. This festival is a way to demonstrate a break from reliance on our own ability. It also acts as a means of recognition of our miserable state as human beings apart from God. These attitudes are the necessary first steps of entering into a relationship with the God of Israel.

So when we get to the physical process of cleaning the leavening out of the house in preparation for Matzah, we can take the time to engage in the process of examining our lives for any vestiges of sin, evil, pride, and arrogance that is hidden away. We then learn of the necessity of discarding these ways of evil from our lives and the ease with which they can creep back in. Moreover, Matzah speaks of discarding any false teachings—removing the teachings of Egypt, the Pharisees, or any other false teachings from our lives. For at least a week we can strive to get back to the pure and unadulterated Word of God and the teaching of the Kingdom of God. We can take this week to allow the pure teaching of the kingdom to take root in our lives so that by the time of Shavu'ot or Pentecost 50 days later, the pure word that was planted at matzah has spread and we and our communities are leavened and built up by the promises of the kingdom of God.

Bread of Affliction

In Deuteronomy 16, when we encounter the Festival of Unleavened Bread again, we read about another name for unleavened bread: the bread of affliction or poverty. The name "bread of affliction" suggests that this is a type of bread eaten when one is lacking or experiencing poverty, but this is not the case. In many passages in the Bible, the only thing that a person is lacking when making matzah is the time necessary for the bread to leaven. Genesis 19 is an example of this as Lot prepares unleavened bread for his angelic visitors when they arrive at his house in Sodom. In the same way, Gideon prepares unleavened bread for his angelic visitor in Judges 6. In both of these cases, visitors arrived without warning and so there was no time to wait for a loaf to finish leavening, even if starter dough had been available. Throughout the Bible, matzah is made in situations when a person is in a hurry. Instead, the title of "bread of affliction" is meant to cause us to think back on the affliction that Israel faced in Egypt under Pharaoh. An affliction that was so great that Israel left quickly. This title should then cause us to think of our own reaction to sin when we find it in our lives.

The Festival of Matzah is so much more than simply a time of denial, or an excuse to go through the motions of obedience without any deeper impact on our lives. Matzah is a time of reflection and introspection as we strive to eliminate worldly ways and cultivate the things of God's kingdom in our lives. We can also approach this festival from the perspective of matzah being the bread of affliction. All sin is affliction. So when we discover sin in our lives, we should hurry to leave it behind and repent. We are moved to humility in light of what has been done on our behalf. And when we consider the original purpose of this holiday and the swift departure of Israel from Egypt, we can understand it as a call to flee from sin without hesitation or preparation. And just as Israel fled towards Mt. Sinai when they left Egypt, we should flee towards a relationship with God.

First-Fruits

This would seem to be the end of the discussion of the festivals, observances, and celebrations that occur at this time of year, but it is not. While Passover and Matzah are the only observances mentioned for this time of year in the book of Exodus, there is another ritual that was to take place during this week. This ritual is an event that is spoken of only once in all of scripture. Unlike Passover and Matzah, it was not a holiday. It was not even a day of celebration or communal gathering. Instead, it was a day in which a sheaf of barley was collected from a field and then brought into the tabernacle or temple and waved by a priest "before the LORD." This event was not a *moed* (appointed time) or a *chag* (festival), and there was no communal involvement or day off of work for this ritual. Rather, this day served as the signal that grain from the new harvest could be eaten by the people of Israel. The event is mentioned in Leviticus 23 and is described as the day that marked the beginning of the fifty-day count to the festival of Shavu'ot:

> And the LORD spoke to Moses, saying, "Speak to the people of Israel and say to them, When you come into the land that I give you and reap its harvest, you shall bring the sheaf of the firstfruits of your harvest to the priest, and he shall wave the sheaf before the LORD, so that you may be accepted. On the day after the Sabbath, the priest shall wave it. And on the day when you wave the sheaf, you shall offer a male lamb a year old without blemish as a burnt offering to the LORD. And the grain offering with it shall be two-tenths of an ephah of fine flour mixed with oil, a food offering to the LORD with a pleasing aroma, and the drink offering with it shall be of wine, a fourth of a hin. And you shall eat neither bread nor grain parched or fresh until this same day until you have brought the offering of your God: it is a statute forever throughout your generations in all your dwellings.
> —Leviticus 23:9-14

Even though the Bible never gives this particular day a name, it has become known as first-fruits. There is some disagreement between Judaism and some Christian groups who observe this day over when it should fall within the week of Matzah. Although it is not explicitly stated in the text, we can infer that this day occurred during the week of Matzah because it marked the start of the count to Shavu'ot. This raises the question of which day the count is supposed to begin. All the text says is the "day after the Sabbath." In Judaism, this is understood to mean the day after the first day of Matzah. You see, in Judaism, and even in the New Testament, the first day of Matzah is referred to as a Sabbath. The first day of Matzah is a day in which all of Israel is to refrain from work, so it has been inferred that this is equivalent to a Sabbath day with some small modifications. But since it is not a weekly seventh-day Sabbath, these days of rest, which are connected to the festivals, are called High Sabbaths. It is because of this convention that the passage in Leviticus 23 is seen as referring to the second day of Matzah. In this view, the day of the sheaf wave offering can be any day of the week, but it will always be the same day on the Hebrew calendar—the sixteenth day of the month of Aviv or Nisan.

As I said previously, some disagree with this interpretation. The text of Leviticus 23 and elsewhere have been examined and it has been recognized that only one of the seven *moedim* is ever called a Sabbath in scripture: Yom Kippur or the Day of Atonement. While many of the other festivals include a day or two off of work, only Yom Kippur is explicitly called a Sabbath in the Hebrew Scriptures. Because of this, the assertion is made that the Sabbath that is referred to in Leviticus 23:11 is the weekly Sabbath. And so the day of the sheaf wave offering can occur on any calendar day between the 15th and the 21st, but it will always be the same day of the week: the first day of the week, the day that we call Sunday. For Christians, this makes sense as Jesus was raised as the first-fruits of those who have fallen asleep, as Paul states in 1 Corinthians 15:20, and He rose on the first day of the week. If we understand it this way, then there has always been a day in the Hebrew calendar that foreshadowed the resurrection of the Messiah.

Regardless of which way you choose to understand this passage, some things are clear. First, this particular day is not a festival in the

Hebrew Scriptures. While it takes place during the Festival of Matzah, it is not considered a festival in the same way as the other events listed in Leviticus 23. Second, this observance was not something that was accomplished by the community of Israel. Rather, this particular day is accomplished solely by priests. This was not a general observance other than that the new crops for the year were not to be eaten until after this wave offering was accomplished.

Regardless of these facts, this day has become one of celebration for Christians. This was the day that Jesus rose from the dead. Because of this, this day has become one of our greatest days of celebration. The grave was opened, death was defeated, and Jesus became the first-fruits of the resurrection on this day. In many ways, this day that is relatively lost in the pages of the Torah has become the most significant day of celebration for those who are in Jesus.

The Themes of Passover

In Colossians 2:17, Paul calls the festivals, new moons, and Sabbaths, shadows of things to come. This verse has often been used to dismiss the importance of these things, but if we stop and consider the text, this metaphor should actually enhance their importance. Consider it: all things that are in the presence of a light source cast a shadow. Shadows cannot be separated from the substance that casts them or from the source of the light. Both the light and the substance work together to create the shadow. With all three parts examined together as a whole, we can gain a much clearer picture of the fullest expression of the reality of our Messiah as each part works together to ensure that no mistakes are made. So the question arises, how do we find these shadows of the Messiah in these events, the feasts, new moons, and Sabbaths? Well, we have already engaged in this practice to some degree. Every time we look at the symbolism of an item or explore a Biblical metaphor we engage in this practice of examining the shadows of the Messiah, and in so doing, we learn more about Him, His mission, and His Kingdom. But there are other ways to discover shadows of the Messiah besides these.

One of the more powerful ways to develop the shadows contained in as part of the Bible is to examine the occurrence and recurrence of themes. Themes are powerful because they allow us to connect various passages that are scattered throughout the many pages of scripture. In these connections, we discover underlying eternal principles. Recognition of Biblical themes is a powerful tool that can bring the Bible to life in previously unimagined ways. With this tool at our disposal, we can discover the power in Passover that can propel this event from simply a memorial meal into one of the most foundational events in our own lives. Once we see them we will discover that the themes of Passover occur throughout the Bible and are foundational to our faith. These themes will then reveal a new and profound depth to this ancient book that can truly improve your walk with God.

Please understand that this exploration of the themes of Passover is not exhaustive. I may have missed themes that are part of Passover, although I did my best to get the most vital. I also did not get every theme in the Bible. There are many themes present in the Bible, but not all of them are part of Passover. Likewise, some themes are part of the book of Exodus and the entire Exodus journey that I also skipped over as they are not specifically related to the Passover other than tangentially. If you have never been introduced to the concept of Biblical themes before, I pray that this section of this book serves as the fuel to begin your pursuit of this amazing Bible study tool.

Finally, as I was writing this portion of this book I was two drafts in before I recognized something that blew my mind. When I started this section on themes I approached each of these themes in isolation.

Each was its own little essay that often overlapped the other themes but really had no true dependence on each other. But as I went through this text again I realized that the themes that I had already identified and written on for several weeks did indeed work together in sets of three. What I found even more fascinating was that these sets of three each then work together to point to an even greater overarching application that is foundational to the Biblical story. So as we go through this portion of the book I will be exploring these themes in this way, in sets of threes and I have chosen to name these sets Tri-themes. Each tri-theme will have its own focus that will be wrapped up after each theme is explored individually.

Tri-theme One: Living as Subjects: Persecution

The themes of Passover begin with a harsh reality for anyone who would call themselves a Christian and live according to the standard of Christ. It is the way that Israel lived at the beginning of the book of Exodus. As the book begins, Israel lived under an increasingly oppressive regime. This oppression was initiated by a King who had forgotten the history between the two nations of Israel and Egypt. Pharaoh saw Israel as a people who did not owe allegiance to him and who, under the right circumstances, could become a threat. So this king did everything that he could to subjugate this group of people that he perceived as a threat.

When we move out of the Torah and begin to read further, we find similar stories of oppression and persecution throughout the Bible. We don't even have to leave the book of Exodus or get to Mt. Sinai before attempts at persecution begin again. Exodus 17 recounts the story of the Amalekites attacking Israel as they made their way to Mt. Sinai.

The newly freed nation of Israel was traveling into a wilderness away from all civilization, and the Amalekites, as best as we can tell, acted out of fear and hatred of this new nation. As a result, Amalek attacked Israel, and they were forced to defend themselves. In this fight, as long as Israel depended on their own power they lost, but when they focused on God for their defense, they were victorious. Later, Deuteronomy 25 adds that when the Amalekites attacked, it was the weak and tired, those who were lagging behind, that were targeted among Israel. Not the warriors, strong, and healthy. Instead, it was those who had become separated from the protection of the group that were the first to fall.

Then in the book of Numbers, the Moabites and Midianites hire a prophet to curse Israel on their behalf. Once again, Israel is perceived as a threat to a nation that Israel was not intending to do any harm. The king of Moab, however, feels threatened and so Balaam is hired to weaken Israel should it come to war. In the course of the story, Balaam is unable to curse Israel and the king of Moab gets angry at him. So rather than attempting to weaken Israel from outside, Balaam instructs the king of Moab on how to get Israel to curse themselves by simply placing temptations in their path. Again, a nation outside of Israel sought to bring Israel into subjection, this time through enticement to disobedience.

As the story of Israel continues in the book of Judges, the nations outside of Israel are at a near-constant state of war with Israel. For many decades on end, Israel would come under one oppressor or another until God would raise up a judge to deliver Israel.

David was oppressed by Saul, his sworn liege. Elijah and the prophets of God were pursued and persecuted by Jezebel, the queen of Israel, and the prophets of Ba'al. Jeremiah was thrown in a pit and left to die because he dared speak truth to those in power. Jesus was drug through a series of farce trials before being hung on a cross to die, and only one of His disciples died of old age, and him after being boiled in oil and exiled according to the tradition surrounding him. The rest were executed at the hands of mobs and governments.

Persecution and oppression are a way of life that many of us in the West do not appreciate or truly experience and this persecution has become one of our greatest fears. The New Testament states in several places (Matthew 10:22, Matthew 24:9, John 15:20, 2 Timothy 3:12) that persecution is the expected response of the world (Egypt) to those who belong to God (Israel).

> Indeed, all who desire to live a godly life in Christ Jesus will
> be persecuted, while evil people and impostors will go on
> from bad to worse, deceiving and being deceived.
> —2 Timothy 3:12-13

The reality of persecution and oppression for the people of God is a central part of Passover. It is the bitter herbs that are part of the memorial meal that acts as a reminder of this persecution. Accepting the sacrifice of the lamb is the equivalent of signing up for persecution in one form or another. Thus, as part of the meal, we willingly eat of the bitterness of oppression. As modern Western Christians who live in countries of relative peace towards believers, engaging in Passover can remind us that the state of affairs that we experience is not the norm. The relative peace that we have is not eternal. When oppression or persecution comes upon us in any form, it should not surprise us. Instead, it should remind us of our calling to a kingdom that is not of this world.

Tri-theme One: Living as Subjects: Tyranny

On the flip side of the oppression coin are those who engage in and enforce the oppression—the enemy that seeks to control Israel and keep them powerless. This enemy knows that if Israel is occupied with constant labor and is forced to spend every moment on survival, then they would be in no place to rise against him. Once again, we find this to be a central theme in Scripture, as throughout its history Israel found itself languishing under a tyrannical master.

Each of the examples of persecution in the previous theme occurred at the hands of tyrants both petty and large. Often this tyranny is simply an attempt to subdue the people of God, but there are plenty of cases when their tyrant gains the upper hand and truly oppresses the people of God. There is Shalmaneser of Assyria, Nebuchadnezzar of Babylon, or even the aforementioned Jezebel, one of several tyrants who gained the throne in Israel. Even Solomon is described as being oppressive to the people of Israel in both harsh labor and oppressive taxes (1 Kings 12).

The worst offender in the opinion of many is Antiochus Epiphanes of the Seleucid Empire in the second century BCE. While this time of Israeli history is not specifically recorded in the Bible, the books of Maccabees describe what life was like under this oppressive regime.

So in the first century, when Jesus came as the Messiah amid the oppression of the Roman Empire, the people assumed that He had come to free Israel from this tyranny and all future tyrants in fulfillment of the Passover story. But Jesus had different plans. He recognized that there is a greater enemy of mankind than any human government. Jesus identified the tyrants of sin and death and the personification of these ideals in the character of Satan as the enemy. This is the enemy that He came to conquer, not Rome or Greece.

In Ephesians 6 Paul echoes the sentiment that the true oppressor of mankind is not a government or the leaders of any particular group of people, but that the true oppressor of men is spiritual.

> For we do not wrestle against flesh and blood, but against the rulers, against the authorities, against the cosmic powers over this present darkness, against the spiritual forces of evil in the heavenly places.
> —Ephesians 6:12

Through the ministry of Jesus, the curtain of reality was pulled back and we were given a glimpse of the greater reality that Passover only hints at. There is a spiritual enemy of mankind that seeks to enslave and destroy. In Jesus's true fulfillment of Passover, He destroyed the greatest enemy that mankind has ever known.

Jesus fulfilled this deliverance by defeating the gods of the world as in Exodus 12:12. The judgment that was enacted on Egypt was not only a judgment on the people who were oppressing Israel but also a judgment on the gods that Egypt worshiped. These are the same gods that led Egypt to take dehumanizing action against their fellow human beings. And these gods are the same principalities and powers that Paul calls the true enemy of the people of God in Ephesians 6. It is these gods that serve the greater enemy of sin and death. Sin and death are the greatest tyrants of all mankind. Those who serve these tyrants often become tyrants in their own right as they act in the image of the gods that they serve.

And what is to be the Christian response to this tyranny that we find in Passover and elsewhere? Submit. Romans 13 spells it out clearly. Submission to the proper authorities of government is what the believer is called to. Even if these representatives are tyrannical.

Submit to them even if they seek to enslave or destroy us. During persecution from human tyrants, we are to apply the blood of the lamb to our lives. This then frees us as individuals and communities from the greater enemy, and gives us the greater hope and promise that God will judge righteously one day. If we find ourselves in this situation we are to stand back and allow God to work for our salvation. And if that means that we die while in submission to tyrannical authority? Well, read the section on the previous theme. That is our lot and our calling. They killed our Lord and Savior after all. If these powers gain authority over us, they will kill us as well. We should refuse to conform to their expectations, but we must still submit to the proper authorities, even if they are tyrannical.

Tri-theme One: Living as Subjects: Freedom

The third piece of this tri-theme is the theme of slavery—heavy labor to the point of no rest. No time off, no breaks, no ability to refresh. Every moment spent in service to the masters of this world. So many fall into this trap. You must work without a break to satisfy the taskmaster, to create something for yourself, to accumulate physical goods, to put food in your belly, to keep the creditors at bay. In the end, conforming to the masters of this world will result in the things you own, owning you. In service to them, there is no rest. Once again, this is the natural condition of man before an encounter with God and the redemption that follows.

> What then? Are we to sin because we are not under law but under grace? By no means! Do you not know that if you present yourselves to anyone as obedient slaves, you are slaves of the one whom you obey, either of sin, which leads to death, or of obedience, which leads to righteousness? But

thanks be to God, that you who were once slaves of sin have become obedient from the heart to the standard of teaching to which you were committed, and, having been set free from sin, have become slaves of righteousness. I am speaking in human terms, because of your natural limitations. For just as you once presented your members as slaves to impurity and to lawlessness leading to more lawlessness, so now present your members as slaves to righteousness leading to sanctification.

—Romans 6:15-19

Paul describes the life of a human as one of service to one master or another. There is no option of living an autonomous life. All must serve. All must work. There is the master of sin which leads to death. This is the one master which will not let you go. He will force you to slave away and will destroy everything that truly matters to you in the process. Or there is the master of God who frees you from tyrannical enslavement and can bring you into service to a kingdom of righteousness and life. While He is still a master and you must still serve and work, this master is kind. In this life, you will serve a master, but the master Jesus is a kind master whose yoke is not unbearable or heavy.

Into this dynamic of the constant work of service, God commands a day of rest. Israel does not even get to Mt. Sinai before the command comes down to keep the Sabbath in Exodus 16. As we saw earlier, the Sabbath command in Deuteronomy 5 directly connects the keeping of the Sabbath as a day of rest for everyone, including those who live in physical servitude to others. Israel, who had been slaves in Egypt without a day of rest were commanded to cease for one day in seven. In the command of the Sabbath, we find the first taste of freedom for Israel and a physical practice that is the shadow of the hope that we have of new creation. No longer was Israel required to work every day to simply stay alive. Under this new master, everyone was able to take a day to rest from their labor. With the Sabbath, life is no longer defined by what you do to earn a living. Life becomes about who you serve.

Additionally in the ceasing of action that is accomplished in the Sabbath, we catch a glimpse of the gospel according to faith. Salvation is not accomplished through the work of our hands. It is not what we do that creates a way for our eternal survival. Our provision and salvation are found solely in the hands of God. It is His work that brings salvation. Even further, the Sabbath points us to the day when sin and death will be defeated once and for all. A day that is "all Sabbath" as the 11th century Rabbi, Rashi, termed it. The time of the new creation as described in Isaiah 65 and Revelation 21—the hope of complete freedom that all believers look forward to in the New Creation.

Living as a Subject

With these three themes working in concert, we gain insight into the reality of this world. We must live in service to a master, and in reality, there are only two. There is the master of life that wishes to see you live in freedom from the oppression and slavery of the tyrant of death. Or there is the tyrant of sin and death. You must pick one to serve. You cannot serve both.

But understand this: the governments of this world are in service to the tyrant. No matter where your nation falls in the ranking of the freest countries on the earth, your nation is subject to the tyrant of sin and death. Knowing this, then, we can all expect that one day we will be persecuted for our faith. Whether it is a national government or an opposing faction, we will be persecuted. The surprise should not be that we might find ourselves as subjects to an oppressive regime or the target of someone who seeks to destroy our ability to minister. The surprise should be when we find ourselves on our death bed and find that we have been fortunate enough to live in a time and place where this persecution did not come to our doorstep.

But in the meantime, when and if oppression comes down on our heads, our duty is that of Israel in Egypt. We are to be subjects of the evil empire. This does not mean that we conform to the wishes of the tyrant in all things. Rather this means peaceful non-compliance to the tyrant when his desires conflict with the desires of our true master in heaven. Because we are free. We are free from sin. We are free of death, and when we truly believe this, then there is nothing that the tyrants of this world can do to harm us.

Tri-theme Two: The War for Creation: Death

We are mortal beings. Every one of us will die one day, this fact is inescapable. Death is as much part of the human condition as breathing or eating. It is simply a fact of life, albeit a fact that we often attempt to avoid. No one wants to be reminded of their own mortality (sorry for that by the way). It often seems as if it would be better to simply have death strike us out of the proverbial blue, taking us by surprise than it would be to contemplate the reality of our death. Sure, we are going to die, but why think about it before it happens? There are a billion options available to take our minds off this reality. And yet, if you are human, you have been touched by death.

As I write this I am forced to stare death in the face. My family has moved in with my in-laws to care for my wife's grandmother who was recently put on hospice. The nurse left only a few hours ago letting us know that she only has, at most, a few days left. Death is coming to our house and it is coming soon and we all know it. There is no escaping. The destroyer haunts these halls.

In a way, it is fitting that I am writing this book under these circumstances, as death is such a central theme in Passover. In Exodus, Egypt was killing the children of Israel. They were forcing Israel into a half-life of utter desperation and taking any reward that might come from their labor. Then Passover happened, the tables turned, and death was unleashed on the populace of Egypt. The only escape from this death was to partake in a form of death vicariously. A young animal in the prime of its life had to die to prevent this coming death from finding a human victim in their homes.

But the shadow of death is not simply found in the events of that night. The text of the story and the way that it is told reveal a symbol for death that is central to the story. This symbol is introduced in Genesis 12:10. The first time that anyone in Scripture travels to Egypt.

When Abram first went to Egypt, the action that he took to get there is described as "going down." The Hebrew word used in this verse is the word yarad (ירד), which means not only to "go down" but to "descend" or "decline."[7] This word is not talking about the fact that Egypt is south of Israel on a map. This word is speaking of a spiritual descent into a lower place. If we then move through the Bible and examine every instance of someone going to Egypt we will find that in every case the same word is used. Alternatively, when we read of someone leaving Egypt, they are always described as going up, ascending out of Egypt.

It is often presented in Christian teachings that Egypt is representative of the world and there is a measure of this found in the symbol

---

7   Brown, Driver, Briggs and Gesenius. "Hebrew Lexicon entry for Yarad". "The NAS Old Testament Hebrew Lexicon".

of Egypt as used in the Bible. I have even hinted at it previously in this book. But this is not the whole story. Abram was not descending into the world from a place outside of the world in Genesis 12.

What was Abram's great fear as he descended into Egypt with his beautiful wife? When they see you they will kill me, and so Abram disguises himself as the brother of his wife. Then Joseph is sold into slavery. What was the first option that the brothers wanted? They wanted Joseph dead. Instead, he descends to Egypt. When Israel is standing on the edge of the Sea as the armies of Pharaoh approached, what was the complaint of Israel to Moses? "Is it because there are no graves in Egypt that you have taken us away to die in the wilderness?" Egypt isn't best pictured as a symbol of worldliness. Rather, this language is meant to steep Egypt in the symbol of the grave. More specifically, Egypt is depicted in the Bible as a symbol of Sheol, the ancient Hebrew place of the dead.

What is it that ancient Egypt was known for? We see it even today! Egypt was known for its graves. The monuments, tombs, and mummies that are such a huge part of Egyptian archeology were the reality of ancient Egypt. The vast amount of time and energy that was spent building graves in Egypt is incomprehensible to modern people. It was Egypt that perfected the practice of embalming and mummification. Egypt worshiped Anubis, the god of death, and it is from Egypt that we get the "Book of the Dead." The entire culture of Egypt was wrapped around the concept, preoccupation, and worship of death. So when Israel lived in Egypt they were not simply living in the world. They were symbolically living in the place of the dead, and they were slaves to the dead.

When we then turn to the New Testament we find this same set of ideas being described in the epistles. Romans 6:16 which was quoted in the previous section referred to this idea. "You are slaves to the one you serve whether sin, which leads to death or obedience…" Hebrews 2:14-15 echoes this idea: "So that through death He might destroy the one who has the power of death…and deliver those who through fear of death were subject to lifelong slavery." This word picture of Egypt as the place of the dead, and Pharoah as Satan, the one with the power of death is useful in its depiction. It reveals the lengths that Satan will go to to retain His hold over the people of God. But Jesus as our Passover lamb has set us free from this kingdom of death and brought us close to Him.

Tri-theme Two: The War for Creation: Death Defeated

If Egypt is the symbol of death, then what is the alternative? What is the benefit of aligning ourselves with the kingdom of God? Passover shows that when we do so, we receive God's protection from death. Remember, Passover was not a passive action of simply walking past the doors with blood on them. Rather, it was an active defensive action that was taken to prevent the destroyer from entering into the homes of those who had dedicated themselves to God. But who is the destroyer? The destroyer in Exodus 12:12-13 is identified as the LORD. But how can this be since it is the LORD that will act as the protector from the destroyer in verse 23? How can the one who protects from the destroyer in verse 23 and the destroyer of verses 12-13 both be the LORD? The answer to this question requires us to look elsewhere. The first clue is in Deuteronomy:

> See now that I, even I, am he, and there is no god beside me;
> I kill and I make alive; I wound and I heal; and there is none
> that can deliver out of my hand.
> —Deuteronomy 32:39

This passage states that the LORD is the one who determines life and death, and yet, death is the great enemy of mankind. As we will soon discover, the LORD is working to defeat death in the world. Again, how can this be? How can God be the one who brings death, and also be the one who is working to defeat death? Let's go deeper. We gain further insight from the book of Job.

As the book opens, Job is described as righteous and wealthy. Then Satan is introduced, and he is depicted as a member of God's council. Satan and God talk, and during the conversation, Satan claims that the only reason that Job is faithful and righteous is that God protects him from harm. In response to this, God then removes His hand of protection from Job and gives Satan the authority to act in Job's life to do anything to harm him except take his life. Later in chapter 30, Job identifies the LORD as the source of the tragedy that had befallen him, and throughout the book, God never disabuses Job of this notion.

Now you might argue that the story of God and Satan in the heavenly council colluding together to harm Job, as described in the book of Job, should not be taken literally because the book of Job is a work of poetry. But then we find this same idea reflected in 1 Kings 22 and 2 Chronicles 18. Once again, God is in His heavenly council seeking advice on how to entice Ahab to Ramoth-Gilead so that he can be killed there. Again a spirit comes to God and offers to be a "lying spirit" to entice Ahab to take this trip that was needed. Neither Kings nor Chronicles are poetic and they reveal the same setup of a heavenly council. These two episodes give us insight that can help us with this conundrum.

These statements that are made in Exodus 12 that seem to be contradictory descriptions of God, can be understood as a series of commands that have been passed down from the heavenly throne room. This would be similar to Nebuchadnezzar saying, "I have built Babylon" (Dan. 4:30), when in fact we all know that it was the people who served him that accomplished this feat. These seemingly contradictory statements of "I will destroy" and "I will protect from the destroyer" are speaking of God's sovereignty. They are meant to demonstrate His authority over life and death.

So in the Exodus, God unleashed the great enemy that the authors of the Bible identify as death, upon the land of Egypt. This action was taken by God as an act of judgment on a nation whose entire society worshiped and dealt death. Then God also acted to defend Israel from this enemy whom He had unleashed into their midst. Both actions can be seen as commands that were issued by the throne of God to servants who then carried out the commands.

One place we can look to confirm that this type of language is common is in Ezekiel 9. In this chapter, God calls for servants to come and he commands one to mark those who are righteous. Then the other servants are then sent to kill all of those without the mark. A scenario that is very reminiscent of the Passover in many ways. In response to this Ezekiel cries out in "Will You [the LORD] destroy all of Israel in your wrath," to which God responds in verse 10, "my eye will not spare, nor will I have pity; I will bring their deeds upon their heads." This same type of language from Exodus 12. "I will destroy." "I will spare." We see clearly in Ezekiel that it was servants that carried out the actual judgment at God's command. Thus, the King of all can state without equivocation, "I have done this."

When we return to the Exodus, in chapter 14 the armies of Egypt were held back from Israel by a pillar of fire that stationed itself between Israel and their pursuers. Then again, the chaotic waters of death were held back from destroying Israel. Immediately after Israel passed they were unleashed upon the enemy that pursued. Throughout the story, those who acted as agents of death had death visited upon them, and it was God that protected His people from that death when the moment of Exodus came.

With that, let's turn to the New Testament. In its pages, we find that death is once again depicted as the great enemy. It is this destroyer that visits all men (Heb. 9:27), and it is this destroyer that was thrust upon Jesus on the cross. Once again, death was defeated as Jesus rose from the dead. But then, death was not defeated forever. We are again promised that death will one day be defeated once and for all in the future. For now, we wait in expectant hope for that day, knowing that we who are in Messiah Jesus will get to participate in this future kingdom of life:

> For as in Adam all die, so also in Christ shall all be made
> alive. But each in his own order: Christ the first-fruits, then
> at his coming those who belong to Christ. Then comes the
> end, when he delivers the kingdom to God the Father after
> destroying every rule and every authority and power. For he
> must reign until he has put all his enemies under his feet. The
> last enemy to be destroyed is death.
> —1 Corinthians 15:22-26

The Bible opened with the release of death upon the world as Adam chose to know good and evil, rather than to remain faithful and obedient and eat from the tree of life. In Revelation 20-21 we read of the eventual and permanent defeat of death in the world. But here in the Passover, in both the Old and New Testament, we see this process in action. Only those who are protected by the blood of the lamb will escape the permanence of death and cross over into life.

In the age of Messiah, this hope of the defeat of death becomes central to our faith. We as believers in the Messiah are to identify with the death of Jesus and accept His death on our behalf. In identifying with the death of the Messiah we willingly accept the death of the flesh in exchange for the greater life that is the hope of New Creation. This is what we participate in when we go through the ritual of baptism. The death and resurrection of our Messiah are acted out as we pass through the water, and on the other side, we are a new creation.

Tri-theme Two: The War for Creation: New Creation

When Paul speaks of salvation in 2 Corinthians 5:17, he states emphatically that all who are in Christ are a new creation. The old is gone and the new has come. But just how is this depicted in Passover?

When Israel entered Egypt during the days of Joseph they were a family. Thay are described as a clan, or a series of clans connected through familial ties, who uprooted themselves and moved to a new and foreign place. While in Egypt this was all that Israel was. They were simply a family. While in Egypt they grew to be a large family to be sure, but they were still only a family. Exodus begins with this reminder in Exodus 1:1-6. During this time in Egypt, they were not autonomous. They were under the authority of the Egyptian regime and subjects of the Egyptian king.

So when the Passover occurred and Israel was set free, no longer were they a collection of clans that were united by kinship, rather they were birthed into the world as a collective new creation—a nation that was in covenant with God:

> Now therefore, if you will indeed obey my voice and keep
> my covenant, you shall be my treasured possession among all
> peoples, for all the earth is mine; and you shall be to me

> a kingdom of priests and **a holy nation**. These are the words
> that you shall speak to the people of Israel.
> —Exodus 19:5-6

As Israel left Egypt and traveled together into the wilderness, their status in the world changed. They entered the world stage as a nation among nations. More than a family, rather, Israel was something completely new. And this brand new nation was unique as it was led by and was in covenant with the God of creation. Israel became a thing that had never before existed on the earth—truly they were a new creation.

This theme is significant because it describes what happens to each one of us when we take on the sacrifice and the blood of the lamb:

> Therefore, if anyone is in Christ, he is a new creation. The old
> has passed away; behold, the new has come.
> —2 Corinthians 5:17

We don't, in the moment of salvation, gain a new body, new thoughts, or new personality. Our memories are the same, our friends and family tend to stay the same (although rejection from them does occur), our habits and personal likes and dislikes remain our own. Yet Paul states that in that moment of redemption the one who has been redeemed is a new creation. A new person with new goals and motivations replaces the person who was previously there. No longer are we motivated by our flesh, nor are the things of this world our goal. Upon salvation, the Christian is now aligned with the kingdom of God and has entered into His nation. We reject the kingdoms of this world and ultimately the kingdom of sin and death. We have become something new, something that the world did not witness before the death of Jesus. Upon our salvation we are entered into a kingdom without borders; a kingdom that is not defined by race or language. Instead, we are part of the new creation of the kingdom of God. And just like Israel at the time of the Exodus, this kingdom is a kingdom that is defined solely by our allegiance to the God that we serve.

Just as Israel became a symbol of new creation in the Exodus, so too the new creation of the Christian becomes a symbol of an even greater reality that we still look forward to. As we read the prophetic books of Isaiah and Revelation, the end result of history, past and future, is a universal new creation. It is a new way of being that the current creation yearns for—a day when the rules change and death is defeated once and for all. It is a day without weeping, hunger, or violence. So too, the new creation of a life saved by Jesus becomes a microcosm of the greater recreation that is to come. And this microcosm is found occurring in the events surrounding Passover and salvation.

The War for Creation

Since the day that Adam ate from the forbidden fruit in the Garden of Eden, death has stalked mankind. Humanity has been helpless to fight against this great destroyer of lives, hopes, and dreams. We do our best with science and medicine but the best that we have been able to accomplish is to simply delay the inevitable. Death will one day claim each of us. There is no stopping it. Unless there is.

While we are helpless to stop or reverse death, there is one who is not. The God who initially created a world without death has purposed to work through history to create a means by which death can be made powerless. Death has been defanged, and its sting has been removed. We have been presented in the resurrection of Jesus as a sign of things to come.

No longer is mankind helpless in the face of death. Through Jesus, we find assurance that death has been overcome. He has passed through death and come out the other side victorious. He has made a promise to us that if we join ourselves to Him, death will not be a permanent state of affairs. Instead, we can become part of the new creation in which death will be no more. With this assurance and the hope of a future in which there will be no more death, we can now face death with courage because we know that it is ultimately powerless to those who are in the Messiah Jesus.

Tri-theme Three: God Introduced: Judgment

I had a conversation with someone once who stated that they view the God of the Old Testament as being judgmental and vengeful, while they see the God of the New Testament as a God of love. This has often been presented to me as a caricature of what some believe about how the Bible presents God, but this was the first time that I had encountered someone who voiced this opinion as his own. It occurred to me later while I was reflecting on the exchange, that while portions of the Old Testament—such as the flood or Passover or the Babylonian Exile—do make up a large chunk of the gripping stories of the Old Testament, these events are an outpouring of one of the greater character traits of God: His justice.

Again, we have already touched on this topic, but the rabbit hole always seems to go deeper. When we read these passages of judgment on mankind we often find that there is a judgment-in-kind that is being accomplished. This has already been explored in the destruction of the firstborn being repayment for the destruction of the sons of Israel. Or the plundering of Egypt as back payment for the labor that Israel had done on behalf of Egypt. But it doesn't stop here. We can find this pattern of judgment-in-kind throughout all of the stories of judgment that we read in the Bible.

Take the narrative of the flood as an example. In Genesis 6, we read about the condition of the earth before the flood and the resulting judgment that God calls down on the earth:

> And God saw the earth, and behold, it was **corrupt**, for all flesh had **corrupted** their way on the earth. And God said to Noah, "I have determined to make an end of all flesh, for the earth is filled with violence through them. Behold, I will **destroy** them with the earth.
> —Genesis 6:12-13

Now we miss it in English, but there is a judgment-in-kind stated in this verse. The word that is translated as "corrupt" in verse 12 is the word *Shachat* (שחת). *Shachat* is what the earth was because of the actions of men. And so, in verse 13, God declares that He will destroy the earth as an act of Judgment upon the corrupt earth. But the word translated as "destroy" in verse 13 is also the word *shachat*. It is as if the text is saying, "The earth was corrupted by all flesh, and so God was going to corrupt the perpetrators of this corruption with the earth." The flood that we then read of is the outpouring of God's justice-in-kind on mankind.

We find a similar thing occurring in the time of the Exile of Judah into Babylon. Throughout the age of the kings, Israel was on a trajectory to abandon the worship of the LORD. All through 1 and 2 Kings, we read about the two nations of Israel increasingly turning to the worship of other gods. These books recount story after story of Israel abandoning and forsaking the LORD for the gods of the nations. And so this is the justice that was declared for Israel.

> And when your people say, 'Why has the LORD our God
> done all these things to us?' you shall say to them, 'As you
> have forsaken me and served foreign gods in your land, so you
> shall serve foreigners in a land that is not yours.'
> —Jeremiah 5:19

Again we read of a judgment-in-kind for transgression occurring in the justice system of God. They abandoned God to serve other foreign gods at home, and so He abandoned them to serve foreign men in their homes. This principle is applied throughout scripture when it comes to God's judgment. We see it stated clearly as early as Genesis 4:14 and as late as Revelation 13:10. With one of God's qualities being justice as described in Exodus 34:6-7, then we must recognize and accept that the quality of justice necessitates judgment. And this did not cease at the death of Jesus. Rather, it continues to this day, and we see this most clearly in the book of Revelation.

God as described in the New Testament did not give up on His quality of justice in exchange for the quality of love. Rather He acts in a way that perfectly balances both justice and love at all times. These qualities are not opposites of each other, they are complementary to each other. There is, in reality, no difference between how God acts before and after Jesus. Malachi 3:6, James 1:17, Hebrews 13:8, and other passages repeat that God does not change. He is the same and acts the same at all times. Rather, we must recognize that justice is a quality that flows out of love. In God's love for victims, the poor, the oppressed, and the downtrodden, His nature requires that judgment be visited upon those who are perpetrators.

So in the grand cosmic justice system of the universe, Jesus who did no wrong accepted the penalty due for sin. He took on judgment so that we might live. In doing so He created a way for mankind to accept the judgment of death without the killing of the body. Then through this acceptance of God's justice visited upon the Messiah, we can put to death the body of sin that we inhabit and begin to act in the manner of new creation. The old man dies and a new man is raised in his place to live out the reality of our great hope. Death defeated forever and resurrection into a world without sin and death.

Tri-theme Three: God Introduced: Sovereignty

Why does the LORD have the right to sit in judgment over the inhabitants of the earth? Why was He justified to engage in mass death events such as the flood, the destruction of Sodom and Gomorrah, or Passover? What gives Him the right? Well as we search the pages of Scripture it becomes clear that it is because He is the King over all creation. Psalm 47 is a song that declares this idea. More specifically, it is the last half of the Psalm that repeats this truth over and over.

> Sing praises to God, sing praises! Sing praises to our King,
> sing praises! For God is the King of all the earth; sing praises
> with a psalm! God reigns over the nations; God sits on his
> holy throne. The princes of the peoples gather as the people
> of the God of Abraham. For the shields of the earth belong to
> God; he is highly exalted!
> —Psalm 47:6-10

He is King of the earth. He reigns over the nations. He sits on His holy throne. He is the King of kings and Lord of lords. As king, He must rightly judge His subjects that inhabit His domain. To serve as the protector of the weakest of His subjects and prosecute those who would transgress His law. We see that God's actions in scripture demonstrate that He is not just a judge, but also acts in all the ways a king would. He is a lawgiver, provider, the one who imposes order. He surrounds Himself with counselors, fights for and protects His people, and defeats the enemies of His kingdom.

Upon examination of the plagues inflicted upon Egypt, we can see a consistent theme emerge: the LORD is the King of the earth. He is not just the king over the created things of the world and physical matter; He also rules over the weather, the lights in the sky, and the very essence of life and death itself. If a person were presented with no other part of the story of Israel but the Passover they would be forced to acknowledge that this story demonstrates the authority and power of the LORD—His power over water (water to blood and the Red Sea), the earth (dust turned to gnats), animals (frogs and death of livestock), and the heavens (hail, winds that bring locusts, and darkness). The ultimate expression of his authority and power is seen in his precise control over who lives and who dies in every household, regardless of which deity that household worships. Throughout Scripture, the LORD is depicted as a king, and this narrative demonstrates His power and authority over all of creation.

Tri-theme Three: God Introduced: Faithfulness

God is faithful. This is a unifying tenant of the Christian faith. Regardless of how messed up reality seems or how treacherous men can be, ultimately God is faithful. Once again, the Passover narrative provides a glimpse of this truth.

While I have already covered this topic, it deserves to be part of this list. In the case of Passover, we read of a promise that was made to Abraham when God cut a covenant with him in Genesis 15:13-14. Part of this covenant was prophecy. Your offspring will be sojourners and slaves for four hundred years. This is simply a truth of the future that God relates to Abram. In the next line, we read of a promise that God made with Abraham: "I will bring them out through judgments, and they will leave with great possessions." So they will become the subjects of an oppressor, but God will deliver them out of this oppression. But wait, there's more! The promise doesn't end here. God continues with an even further promise that He will bring Abraham's offspring into the land of Canaan and give it to them as a possession.

Even earlier in Genesis in chapter 12:2 we read that God promised Abraham to make him into a "great nation," even though his wife was barren. And later in Genesis 17, Abraham is commanded to take the sign of circumcision as he is being told that Sarah will in fact be the mother of his heir.

Each of these we have seen before, but these are not the last time that we encounter the promises of God to bring about what we now call the Exodus. From the beginning of Exodus, when Moses encounters God in the burning bush, God reiterates this promise to Moses:

> Go and gather the elders of Israel together and say to them,
> 'The LORD, the God of your fathers, the God of Abraham,
> of Isaac, and of Jacob, has appeared to me, saying, "I have
> observed you and what has been done to you in Egypt, and I
> promise that I will bring you up out of the affliction of Egypt
> to the land of the Canaanites, the Hittites, the Amorites, the
> Perizzites, the Hivites, and the Jebusites, a land flowing with
> milk and honey."'
> —Exodus 3:16-17

In this surprise personal audience before the God of all creation, before Moses begins to make his way back to Egypt, God reiterates the promise that He made with Abraham. The explanation for why this is the appropriate time for this action can be found in the final three verses of the previous chapter. These last three verses provide the foundation for an even deeper rabbit hole into the nature of God that we will not get into in this book other than in passing.

In Exodus 2:23 the people of Israel call to God for help, and this cry is brought to His attention. In response to this cry, God responds in four ways. First, He hears. Remember back on the discussion of the word shema earlier. Second, He remembered. Again, look back to the previous discussion on the Hebrew word for remember. This is not that God had forgotten, rather it was now time to act in connection to the previous covenant. He saw the people of Israel. Not that He hadn't seen them in their plight, but that now it was time to act in response to what was seen. And God knew. He became intimately involved in what was occurring in Egypt.

This passage is one of the primary places in Scripture that speaks to the nature of God as Omniscient (God knew), Omnipresent (God saw and heard), and Omnipotent (God remembered, or acted in accordance with what had come before).

As we continue in the Exodus, we find another reiteration of the promise of the covenant in Genesis 15 in chapter six. This time the message is given to Moses and He is told to spread this message and declare it to all the children of Israel:

> I also established my covenant with them to give them the land of Canaan, the land in which they lived as sojourners. Moreover, I have heard the groaning of the people of Israel whom the Egyptians hold as slaves, and I have remembered my covenant. Say therefore to the people of Israel, 'I am the LORD, and I will bring you out from under the burdens of the Egyptians, and I will deliver you from slavery to them, and I will redeem you with an outstretched arm and with

great acts of judgment. I will take you to be my people, and
I will be your God, and you shall know that I am the LORD
your God, who has brought you out from under the burdens
of the Egyptians. I will bring you into the land that I swore to
give to Abraham, to Isaac, and to Jacob. I will give it to you
for a possession. I am the LORD.'
—Exodus 6:4-8

Again, we find these promises to deliver and redeem Isreal from
slavery, this time alongside the nature of God as remembering and
seeing. He promises here to become their God, and they, His people.
Alongside this, He restates the covenant of Genesis 15, that He will
bring them into the land and give it as a possession.

The simple fact is that the LORD is presented as a God of covenants in scripture. When He makes a covenant with people, He
ensures that His part of the covenant is accomplished. This facet of
the nature of God is best captured in one Hebrew word, *chesed* (חסד).
This word is one that translators have found difficult to translate con-
sistently in the Bible, and so we find this word translated as goodness,
kindness, lovingkindness, mercy, favor, and even pity in one place.
No one of these English words captures the depth that this Hebrew
word contains because we don't have a singular word that fits the idea
that this word contains. Rather, the true depth of this word is perhaps
best captured by the idea of "enduring loyalty to covenant." This word
provides assurance to those who are part of a covenant with God that
when He makes a promise, He will follow through and make sure it
comes to fruition. A shorter way to express the meaning in this word
is to use the term "covenant loyalty."

When we turn to Exodus 34 and the event on Mt. Sinai when
God passes before Moses and declares His character, *chesed* is one of

the core and defining characteristics in the list. The LORD is a God who makes covenants with men, and He is a God who then carries out the terms of those covenants. It is His own loyalty to His covenants and to His covenant partners that is described as the motivation for why God takes many of the actions He takes throughout Scripture.

Here in Passover this quality is on full display. God's *chesed* ensures that God will be faithful to His promises. This quality is one of the primary character traits of God that is highlighted and praised in the traditional modern Seder. The LORD is a God of covenants and it is because of His loyalty to the covenant that He made with Abraham that Passover occurred. It is that same loyalty to His covenants that provides for our own salvation and redemption today.

God Introduced

It is not possible to fully convey the vastness of God's nature and character in such a brief treatment as the one I have presented. But the fact is that Passover does not reveal the entirety of God's character and nature. This event was simply the introduction to the people of Israel to the God that their ancestors had worshiped. It would take time living in God's presence to learn the full extent of the nature of God.

Israel had lived in Egypt for centuries without any direct revelation of God. All they had were the stories of their ancestors. So when God shows up and promises to deliver, Israel knows very little about this God. The revelation of character that is provided in the course of the plagues and Passover is simply a foundation on which Israel can begin a relationship. It is the first step in a progression of revelation that lasts throughout the rest of the book of Exodus and beyond.

These qualities are an important first step in getting to know the God of Israel. He is the king of all creation, and as such, it is His responsibility to judge mankind. This quality of judgment should produce a measure of fear, and it is the fear of God that is the beginning of wisdom (Proverbs 9:10). But alongside this fear, there is the knowledge that He is faithful to His covenants and promises. These promises then provide a measure of stability and hope in light of a world that seems to be going mad around us. With this knowledge of God, we have a foundation on which we can then begin to build a relationship of trust and respect towards the one who is trustworthy and faithful.

Tri-theme Four: Relationship with God: Dedication

The final plague of the ten, the plague of death on the firstborn, required each household to offer up a sacrifice. We have already explored how that sacrifice was accomplished according to the ancient cultural practice of threshold sacrifices; killing an animal on the doorstep of a house to dedicate that house to a particular god. But why was this action necessary? Well, Israel had been in Egypt for several centuries, and they had likely picked up a lot of the worship practices of the Egyptians during this time. We see this assertion supported in Exodus 32 in the events surrounding the golden calf. While Moses was gone for 40 days the people got antsy and demand that an image be crafted to represent the LORD.

> And he received the gold from their hand and fashioned it
> with a graving tool and made a golden calf. And they said,
> "These are your gods, O Israel, who brought you up out of
> the land of Egypt!" When Aaron saw this, he built an altar
> before it. And Aaron made a proclamation and said, "Tomorrow shall be a feast to the LORD."
> —Exodus 32:4-5

The people believed that they had been abandoned by the representative of God, and thus by God, so they sought to create a new representation. They attempted to capture the essence of God in an image of gold. "These are your gods who brought you out of Egypt," and "tomorrow is a feast unto the LORD." The worship practices of Egypt were so ingrained in Israel at this point that despite having agreed three times to the terms of the Ten Commandments and the commands of Exodus 21-23, in less than forty days, Israel decided that the best course of action was to break the covenant and return to the familiar. They knew how the worship of the gods worked in Egypt and so they applied the same form of worship to the LORD. In taking this action they ended up breaking the second command of the ten. Israel saw themselves as still worshiping the LORD, the dedication to Him that was accomplished through the Passover sacrifice was still in effect in their minds. This calf was not another god. It was the LORD. It was their god! They simply did not know how to worship when they had not yet received instructions on how to do so and so they fell back on what they knew.

Dedication to an entity does not mean simply doing whatever you want in the name of that entity. Dedication means acting in the way that aligns with the one that holds your allegiance. This is something that Israel forgot in their desire to worship. They created a literal sacred cow to accomplish what they desired with no thought about what God wanted from them. As worshippers of the God of Israel, we mustn't fall into the same trap. Dedication and allegiance only matter if we behave faithfully to the one that we are dedicated to. But we must be dedicated to something. Just as we must serve in one capacity or another, we cannot practically serve two masters. If we attempt, at some point our dedication will be revealed when a time of trial and temptation arises. And so, just as Israel applied the blood of a lamb to the doorposts of their house to dedicate their households to the LORD, we too must apply the blood of Jesus to our own lives. It is only through this that we can leave behind the ways of the world and the flesh and become human as God intended from the beginning, and it all starts with a declaration of Allegiance. And this dedication was accomplished through a sacrifice.

Tri-theme Four: Relationship with God: Sacrifice

In modern times, the concept of a blood sacrifice is often misunderstood because it is so foreign to our way of life. Taking an animal and slitting its throat as an act of worship feels dirty to the modern Westerner. But in the ancient world, this was the way that a person worshiped. Animal sacrifice was integral to all forms of worship of nearly every god. It wasn't always an animal that was sacrificed. The range of sacrifice stretches from fruits and vegetables placed at the base of an idol as a means of "feeding" the gods to the greatest sacrifice that a person could give of their sons and daughters—a sacrifice that was seen as greater than giving of one's own life. In the ancient world, sacrifices were used as a means of appealing to various gods for their support in a cause, or as a bribe to get the god to avert their attention away from the worshiper and his cause.

In the Passover sacrifice, we find some of these same ideals being accomplished. The lamb was slain and the blood was applied to the doorpost of the house as an appeal for God to act in defense of the inhabitants of the house. The base assumptions of the ancient form of sacrifice did not change with this initial sacrifice. All that shifted was the god that was being worshiped. It was not until the book of Leviticus that the forms and reasons for sacrifice were changed when it came to the LORD.

The original Passover sacrifice, however, looked very similar to the sacrificial practices of the world. It was accomplished on the threshold of the house. It was accomplished as an act of dedication and as an appeal for protection. This sacrifice would have felt natural to Israel in Egypt in many ways. It wasn't the sacrifice that was important. It was the God that commanded the sacrifice and what the sacrifice meant as a form of dedication that was important. In this sacrifice, Israel was forsaking the gods of Egypt in exchange for the God of Israel.

But we live in a world without blood sacrifices. A world where there is no temple in which to accomplish sacrifice. A world in which our Messiah took on the role of Passover lamb and His blood became how death is turned away from our lives and by which our entry into the Kingdom of God is secured. Our Passover sacrifice has occurred, and yet sacrifice as a concept continues to be part of our experience of worship.

So how are we to engage in sacrifice today if it is not as described in the Torah? I think that the etymology of the English word sacrifice can help us to better understand how this practice can be accomplished today. The word sacrifice in the English language came from the Latin word *sacrificium* in the 12th century. This Latin word is a compound word that is the combination of "sacra," which means "sacred," or "holy," and "facere," which means "to make," or "to do." The word sacrifice means to make something sacred or to do something sacred by giving up something of value. So when we use this word, we must understand that we are attempting to make a thing holy through our sacrifice. We are setting it apart for God's use alone. So if you were to say that you sacrificed sugar for the sake of your health, then you are stating that you are making your health sacred. If you sacrificed Starbucks for a year so that you could afford a vacation, then the vacation is the thing that is being made holy. The sacrifice is the thing that you give up to appease, appeal to, or accomplish the sacred thing. In the Biblical system of sacrifice, animals were killed for the sake of a relationship with the God of creation. In this scenario, God is the thing that is holy and the animals, the worldly wealth, is the thing that was sacrificed.

So when the New Testament speaks of sacrifice it does not do so in the way of blood and animals. It does so in a way that the Levitical sacrificial system only hinted at. The animals simply served as shadows of the true sacrifices that we are to make as part of our worship.

> I appeal to you therefore, brothers, by the mercies of God, to present your bodies as a living sacrifice, holy and acceptable to God, which is your spiritual worship.
> —Romans 12:1

Rather than the life of an animal being given in sacrifice, Paul describes it as if our own lives are to be lived as if we have given our bodies to God in sacrifice. But how do we give our bodies as a sacrifice? Do I go to church and slit my own throat? No! We are not called to kill ourselves in service to our God. Instead, modern sacrifice is accomplished by giving up our desires and will to reveal the holiness of the one that we serve. Through this sacrifice, we can maintain a proper relationship. In Romans 12:1, this sacrifice of ourselves is described in the ESV as "spiritual worship," but in other translations such as the KJV and NET and the Greek text itself, it is described as our reasonable service. The Greek word used here is the word *logikos* (λογικός) which is the origin of our modern word logic. The sacrifice of self is the logical response of a person who has received the gift of salvation. It is this self-sacrifice that helps us to maintain our relationship with God.

As we continue through the New Testament, sacrifice takes on many other forms. In Philippians 4:18, sacrifice is equated to giving of your goods to those who are spreading the gospel. The author of Hebrews likens vocal praise of God to a sacrifice alongside the giving of physical goods to those in need (Hebrews 13:15-16).

While the Levitical system of animal sacrifice has passed with the destruction of the temple and its service, the concept of sacrifice is alive and well today and should be an integral part of our worship practices. We can still sacrifice to maintain a right relationship with God, but the sacrifices that we might engage in begin with our very selves, as this sacrifice is our logical response to the gifts that God has given us.

Tri-theme Four: Relationship with God: Redemption

Most people today associate redemption with the gift of forgiveness that we have been given through Jesus' sacrificial death. Redemption has in many ways become either a religious word or an artistic word—a word reserved for theology, sermons, and prayers, or books and movies and characters. But in the ancient world, the idea of redemption was pervasive. It was the idea of a person being raised from a place of shame into a place of honor. As an example, Joseph was redeemed when he was delivered from prison and made into the second most powerful man in Egypt. As we read the Exodus account, we find in Exodus 6:6 that God intended to redeem Israel from Egypt, and then in Deuteronomy 7:8 we read that God *did* redeem Israel from the house of slavery. Redemption was the thing that God did for Israel at the time of the Exodus.

In the New Testament, Paul speaks of the forgiveness of sins that we have received through the sacrifice of Jesus as a means of redemption (Colossians 1:14, Romans 3:24, etc.), and he also refers to the still coming new creation as the day of redemption (Romans 8:23, Ephesians 4:30, etc). The way that he speaks of redemption is multifold. Redemption is something that has been done for us at the moment of accepting the sacrifice of Jesus, but redemption is also something that will be accomplished for all creation in the future. But what exactly does redemption mean?

If you read what the Old Testament has to say about redemption in the original language you might find something interesting. In Hebrew, two words are translated as redeem or redemption and they each have a slightly different bent on a singular process. The first word is found in Exodus 6:6, and it is used to describe what God was planning to do for Israel:

> Say therefore to the people of Israel, 'I am the LORD, and I
> will bring you out from under the burdens of the Egyptians,
> and I will deliver you from slavery to them, and I will **redeem**
> you with an outstretched arm and with great acts of judgment.
> —Exodus 6:6

The word used in this instance is the word *ga'al* (גאל). This word is a legal term, and it was reserved for the action that a family member would take to lift another out of a bad situation. We find this word used throughout the Torah in cases of levirate marriage (the practice of a man marrying the widow of his brother when the dead brother didn't have any children to carry on his name) in Ruth 3-4. *Ga'al* is also used for redeeming a family member from debt slavery by paying off his debts in Leviticus 25. He was also the kinsman who would be repaid when repayment was judged necessary for a crime but the one that the crime was committed against had died in Numbers 5:8.

Or it was the action that a person takes to reacquire a thing that had previously belonged to God in Leviticus 27.

But this word is not limited to simply lifting a family member out of hardship or inheriting his judgment if it didn't reach him in time. This word is also used to describe the one that would hunt down a person who had killed a family member. In the ancient world, there were no police, and so we read of the process of finding justice for an untimely death in Numbers 35. When a person killed another, whether intentionally or by accident, it was seen as a duty for a family member of the deceased to seek out the killer and kill them in return. This was a form of human initiated justice-in-kind that I spoke of earlier. This position could be occupied by any male of age at any time after the death of their kinsman, and the one in this position had a title. This man was known as the avenger of blood (Deuteronomy 19:6).

So when God tells Moses that he is going to redeem Israel in Exodus 6:6, He is identifying Himself as a kinsman to Israel. He is stepping up to the role of redeemer to deliver them from their servitude. Additionally, He is also taking on the role of the redeemer of blood and delivering the necessary justice to those who had caused the deaths of His family members. It is this kind of vengeance that the slain under the altar call for in Revelation:

> They cried out with a loud voice, "O Sovereign Lord, holy and true, how long before you will judge and avenge our blood on those who dwell on the earth?"
> —Revelation 6:10

But there is another word for redeem that is found in the Torah to describe what happened here in Egypt:

But it is because the LORD loves you and is keeping the oath
that he swore to your fathers, that the LORD has brought you
out with a mighty hand and **redeemed** you from the house of
slavery, from the hand of Pharaoh king of Egypt.

—Deuteronomy 7:8

The word translated as "redeemed" in this verse is the word *Padah*
(פדה). Unlike *ga'al*, this word is not a legal word, and it has no bearing
on the relationships of those involved in the process of redemption.
Instead, this is a general use word that means to ransom or to deliver
a person from a terrible fate. We find this word used five times in
three verses in Numbers 18:15-17 while describing the redemption of
the firstborn. Psalm 55 uses this word to speak of God protecting in
battle, and in Job 5:20 and 6:23 this word is used to describe being
saved from death or the power of a tyrant. This is the word that would
be used when the hero swings in on a rope and rescues the princess
from the pirate king. The hero was not a kinsman of the princess in
this scenario, but he was her redeemer. He did save her and deliver her
from the terrible fate that awaited her at the hands of her oppressor.

Both of these words are used in various places in Scripture to
describe what happened in Egypt. In the Exodus, God acted in the
legal role of a kinsman to Israel and took up the duty to improve
the lives of his family and to repay the dastardly deeds of those who
opposed them. But He also acted in the manner of a hero, paying the
ransom that was due for a hostage, and rescuing them from a terrible
fate with a mighty hand and an outstretched arm.

When we go back to the New Testament, these ideas apply once
again to the redemption that we have in the blood of our Messiah.
He has acted as the kinsman-redeemer, inviting us into His family
through adoption. Then as sons and daughters, we are legally bound

to Him and He is required to act as judge and avenger on our behalf. But at the same time, He acts as a mighty warrior who stood in the face of death and has defeated our great enemy by allowing him to do his worst. Both forms of redemption are aspects of the one redemption that we have in Jesus.

Relationship with God

Relationship with God is something that can be truly humbling to consider. How many people throughout history can say that their king desired to know them personally and intimately? How many can recount how their king swooped in and saved them from certain destruction? How truly honoring is it that the king of all creation has acted on your behalf to save you from certain destruction?

The fact is that not a single one of us is worthy of being in a relationship with the God of the universe, and yet He desires this relationship from us. All that He asks is that we dedicate ourselves to Him above any other contenders. We simply need to declare our allegiance to Him as king.

As part of our declaration of allegiance there is a sacrifice that must be offered, but this sacrifice is not one that we can offer of ourselves. This sacrifice has already been offered, we simply need to accept the sacrifice that has already been made on our behalf. Once this occurs we have been redeemed by the blood of the sacrifice in the past, but which also gives us the hope of witnessing the redemption of creation that is to occur in the future.

As part of the kingdom of God, then our logical response is to give our lives to the one who has bought them. To truly put our will, ideas, well-being, and honor as secondary to the king that we serve. As subjects living in allegiance to our king, His mission then becomes our priority in the world. This priority then means engaging in the process that He has created for our benefit—a process that requires some action on our part.

Tri-theme Five: In Response to God: Cleansing

The month leading up to Passover and the Festival of Matzah is a busy month in our house. During this time we clean every nook and cranny, every drawer, every shelf, the darkest corners of every floor. We do this in preparation for the festival of Unleavened Bread, and some have suggested that it is this preparation that preceded our cultural expression of "spring cleaning."

Now I have already covered the symbol of leaven at some length, and we have already looked at some New Testament scriptures concerning the usage of this symbol by Jesus and the apostles. This symbol is leveraged to encourage the church in Corinth to examine not only their lives, but their local community for any evil, wickedness, or destructive vice so that these things can be removed from their midst. The stated purpose of this examination and subsequent cleansing is so that the community might be capable of worshiping in sincerity and truth. However, this call to action is not just relevant to the church in Corinth, but to each of us individually.

While it is God that cleanses our hearts from sin and cleanses our conscience from condemnation, we find in these exhortations that we have an active role to play in this cleaning process so that we no longer live in the former patterns of our lives. And to this, we turn to the greater symbol of cleansing that we find in the epistles.

> Draw near to God, and he will draw near to you. Cleanse
> your hands, you sinners, and purify your hearts, you dou-
> ble-minded.
> —James 4:8

> Therefore, if anyone cleanses himself from what is dishonorable, he will be a vessel for honorable use, set apart as holy, useful to the master of the house, ready for every good work.
> —2 Timothy 2:21

In both of these verses, we read of an active exercise of cleansing and purifying on the part of the believer. The promise that is given is that He will draw near to you in return if you engage in this process, and you will become useful to Him for the Kingdom. Just like the act of cleansing a house looking for any item that might have been left in the darkest corners, so too, we are to search our hearts and lives for any thought or action that does not align with God or His kingdom.

But this charge does not stop at the individual. Those who find themselves in positions of community leadership are to be aware of the people that worship in their local congregation. When a person is found transgressing one of the four items that are outlined in Acts 15:20-21, then a process is to be initiated. First off, the offender is to be approached privately in the method of Matthew 18, seeking to restore the offender to the congregation through repentance. But if this is not possible, there are a series of escalations until the offender is removed from the community.

The church is not to simply allow those who continue to live in egregious and unrepentant sin to continue to be counted among their numbers. As difficult as it is, this unrepentant and continual sin is to be removed from the midst of the congregation. The leaven is to be cleansed because all it takes is a little leaven to leaven an entire lump.

Tri-theme Five: In Response to God: Baptism

When we think of Christian cleansing rituals it can be easy to import the idea of cleaning yourself into the ritual of baptism, but that is not what this ritual is intended to communicate. Peter states in 1 Peter 3:21 that the waters of baptism are "not a removal of dirt from the body but as an appeal to God for a good conscience." It is not a cleansing. Rather, it is a symbol that serves as a pointer to death and resurrection.

We find in the story of the Exodus a shadow of this practice of baptism. As Israel was fleeing from Egypt, they encountered a place where they could proceed no further. Before them stretched an impassable sea, to each side were towering cliffs, and behind there was an army of chariots bent on their destruction. There was no way out and death seemed inevitable. Then, the mighty hand of God sprang into action in defense of Israel. Behind Israel appeared a pillar of fire blocking their attackers. Simultaneously a wind arose that drove the sea back and dried out the mud and muck of the bottom of the sea to the front. These events allowed Israel to pass through the waters and escape to the other side unscathed, while Israel's enemies perished in the depths of the sea.

When we first encounter this story in the book of Exodus, we don't immediately associate what occurred there in the depths of the sea to the modern ritual of Baptism. However, we find that Paul uses this symbol of the Exodus to explain greater concepts of the gospel:

> For I do not want you to be unaware, brothers, that our
> fathers were all under the cloud, and all passed through the
> sea, and all were baptized into Moses in the cloud and in the
> sea.
> —1 Corinthians 10:1-2

All were baptized into Moses in the cloud and the sea. When the apostle Paul encountered this narrative from the Exodus as he wrote his letter to the church in Corinth, he included this correlation. The children of Israel, when they were redeemed from Egypt, went through an accompanying baptism. The baptism in the sea is termed a baptism into Moses.

But what does it mean to be baptized into Moses? What does it mean to be baptized into any person for that matter? Throughout the New Testament, we find this type of phrasing when it comes to baptism. In Acts 19:3, those who responded to Paul's question of who the believers in Ephesus had been baptized into responded that they had been baptized into John (the Baptist). Paul then goes on to baptize the community into Jesus. In Romans 6:3 and Galatians 3:27, we also read of being baptized into Jesus. But what does it mean to be baptized into a person?

In first-century Judaism, baptism had become a common practice. This practice was something that had morphed over the centuries from the practice of ritual immersion or bathing before entering the temple and had taken on a life of its own. In the book of Leviticus, Israel was taught about the concept of uncleanness and how uncleanness was anathema to the presence of God on earth. As part of this teaching on uncleanness, the status of uncleanness is revealed to be removed through the process of bathing. And so in several places in Jerusalem, mikvahs, or ritual baths were created to facilitate this process.

It wasn't long before mikvahs became commonplace throughout Israel as the process of ritual cleansing began to be practiced for any time that a person felt the need to remove uncleanness whether they were planning on visiting the temple or not. It became common for men to enter the mikvah prior to Sabbath services and morning services. Ritual mikvah immersion was practiced by both men and women for many other reasons, such as preparation for significant life changes, such as entering adulthood, marriage, or for common occurrences such as cleansing away the ritual impurity of the menstrual cycle. Because many of the nations who ruled Israel forbade bathing in the rivers or major sources of water in times before Jesus, the mikvah became a central part of nearly every synagogue and part of many religious practices.

By the first century BCE, the practice of baptism became a popular occurrence in Judaism for yet another purpose. There were many rabbis at this time who began to draw followings of students or disciples. It was common for a new disciple of one rabbi or another to be baptized "into" their chosen rabbi. Baptism became a sign that the student accepted the teacher as their authority and the student would seek to live out their teacher's teachings. If a disciple then changed which teacher or rabbi they followed, they would be baptized once again "into" their new teacher.

So when Paul likens the event in the Red Sea to a baptism "into" Moses, he is making the point that the children of Israel were taking on the authority of Moses to be their leader and teacher. And yet this baptism into Moses did not lead to complete obedience and humility we discover if we continue in 1 Corinthians 10. Rather many were baptized into Moses who acted in rebellion at one point or another as they passed through the wilderness. And this baptism into Moses is juxtaposed in the writings of Paul against the concept of baptism into Jesus:

> Do you not know that all of us who have been baptized into
> Christ Jesus were baptized into his death? We were buried
> therefore with him by baptism into death, in order that, just
> as Christ was raised from the dead by the glory of the Father,
> we too might walk in newness of life.
> —Romans 6:3-4

Baptism into Jesus is a symbolic ritual of identifying ourselves with Him and His teachings, but more than that, it is identifying ourselves with His death and resurrection. Just as Israel was created anew as they passed through the sea and their pursuers were drowned in the heart of the sea, so too our own baptism, when we participate in this ritual, helps us to make a concrete break with who we were in bondage to sin, and to walk in the new creation of life in Jesus. Baptism is, with the foundation of the Christian church, a ritual that is imperative for all who enter into the kingdom of God. Baptism is not a requirement for salvation, but rather it is one of the first acts of obedience to Jesus as Lord and Master. Baptism becomes a matter of identifying ourselves with His death and resurrection.

Tri-theme Five: In Response to God: Testimony

Passing from death to life is a significant experience. The baptism ritual serves as a physical marker in the life of a believer as to that moment of change. It demonstrates that at one point the believer was dead, and now they are alive in Jesus. And that change of status comes with a story.

Nothing captures the human imagination more than a good story. A story is such a powerful tool that one of the most common questions that we encounter when we meet new Christians is a request to hear the story of how this person came to trust in Jesus as their savior. The testimony of a person's journey of salvation is a powerful force in the world. It is so powerful that alongside the blood of the lamb, it is the word of our testimony that allows the believers who are being pursued by the Dragon of Revelation to overcome:

> And they have conquered him by the blood of the Lamb and
> by the word of their testimony, for they loved not their lives

even unto death.

—Revelation 12:11

A true testimony, including the recounting of a life transformed by redemption through the blood of the Lamb and a willingness to sacrifice this life for a greater purpose, can overcome the power of God's enemies.

It is no wonder then that before Israel even left Egypt—before the Passover event occurred—the command came down from on High. Israel was to hold a memorial meal in remembrance of the greatest event of historical significance before the death and resurrection of Jesus. The story of this event is itself a power to be reckoned with. Israel was not even out of the wilderness before Balaak, in fear of Israel, hired Balaam to curse Israel. And again, in the book of Joshua, the inhabitants of Jericho quaked in fear because of the events that had occurred in Egypt. The power of the story of the Exodus and the power of God was felt immediately in the world around them. It was this story that caused fear to manifest in the hearts of those who would stand against God and His chosen people. And for thousands of years, this story served as a witness to Israel of the type and nature of the God they served.

When we get to the New Testament, the story of Passover is morphed by Jesus. Alongside the events of Passover in the year that Jesus died, He instituted another memorial ritual meal—a meal that has been practiced by the Christian church since the very beginning. The night before His crucifixion at the Last Supper, Jesus took the bread and the wine and He taught His disciples to partake of these elements as a memorial of what He was about to do. This was not a replacement of the Passover memorial meal, but rather it served as an enhancement of the meal.

With His death, Passover became something much more meaningful and powerful than simply a story that was told of people that had existed thousands of years before. The story of the Passover became a personal story—a real and vital story that can be told in a billion different ways, and yet it is always the same story. Passover is a story that contains each of the themes that we have already gone through. A person in slavery to the oppressive tyrant of Sin. The death that was the trajectory of their life was defeated and they became a new creation. A very real encounter with God occurred in this story, and in a moment of clarity, the person submitted to the sovereignty of God. They passed under his judgment and accepted His justice because they had witnessed in some real way that He is faithful. A change of allegiance occurred in this life. A personal dedication that was purchased with the ultimate sacrifice. This person who was once in bondage and living in death was redeemed and given a new lease on life.

While the specifics change from person to person, it is in the specifics that all who hear the story learn more about the wondrous compassion, mercy, and grace of our God. In this way, every story is the same as they are all stories of Passover, and yet each is as unique as the person the story belongs to.

After He rose from the dead, Jesus appeared to His disciples and gave them a command. A command to tell the world of what He had done and taught. "Go and make disciples," He told them. "Tell them what I have told you." and then "You will act as witnesses to Me throughout the earth." He states in Acts 1. Go and share the story of the Passover that has come. A Passover that every man, woman, and child can be part of. Go and witness to the whole world of the freedom that has been bought..

What is truly fascinating is that the word for witness in Acts 2 is the Greek word Martus (μάρτυς). This word is the origin of our

English word martyr. A martyr is not simply a person who has died for their faith. A martyr is the witness of a life that cared more for the Kingdom of God than it did for any personal gain. A martyr is a person who has lived Revelation 12:11 to the fullest: "And they have conquered him by the blood of the Lamb and by the word of their testimony, for they loved not their lives even unto death." All who have been redeemed by the blood of the lamb are called to this. We are called to be witnesses to the world of the change that God has accomplished in our lives. We are to speak of His kingdom to the point of death.

For an American or anyone in the West, this might seem a bit drastic. You might think that I am simply being dramatic. I would challenge you to read of the conditions that Christians face in Afghanistan, Iran, China, India, Saharan Africa, and more. Even today men and women give their lives for the gospel, living out Revelation 11:12 in their lives.

Simply consider the disciples. The disciples were charged when Jesus told them of His kingdom and showed them the life-changing power of God. The drastic changes that occurred in their lives echo through the ages to each of us today. Just like the disciples, you have been invited to share about your personal Passover. You have been called to share about the God who made the impossible possible. Your story of death turned to life is important because your story is His story, and this story causes change. The enemy quakes in fear when He hears our stories. So let's tell our stories and participate in spreading new creation throughout the world.

In Response to God

The life of a believer is not their own. We are tasked with engaging in the process of new creation in our own lives. We cannot simply sit back and think that God will do all the work. We must actively take part in the process of growth.

This process of growth is one that occurs on many levels. It is applicable on all scales, from the individual, to the communal, to the uttermost parts of the earth. Every day we should engage in the process of cleaning our lives from the things that do not align with God's kingdom, but let's face it. We are human and this process is long. It is easy to simply coast along without any consideration of the specifics of our lives. God knew this and so He has given us this yearly festival that reminds us of this calling. When Passover approaches we can no longer sit idly by without engaging the world around us in a process of cleansing. We must be aware, though, that this cleansing does not stop in the nooks and crannies of our houses. This process of cleansing must reach into the very depths of our heart.

Likewise, the ritual of baptism is a personal event. We must each engage in this process as a physical reminder of the new life that we have in Messiah Jesus. But our baptism isn't solely a personal affair. Baptism is our first declaration to the world of the life that we have been granted. It serves as our first witness to the world of the God that we serve and the change that has happened within us. But this is just the beginning. After this our lives are to be lives as continual witnesses of our God and His Kingdom to a world that is opposed to this message. Our lives are to be spent in this pursuit, for our lives are no longer our own. We have been purchased at the costly price of one Passover sacrifice.

Changed Identity

When we enter the Kingdom of God, not only are our lives not our own, we are no longer the person that we once were. We have been changed on a fundamental level. Paul speaks of this by using the metaphors of the old man and new man. The old man has been put to death and the new man is to be allowed to reign in our members. This language is used to highlight the nature of the death and resurrection that is part of becoming a new creation in Messiah. The change in a person does not end there though. There is a full change of identity that is included as part of becoming a new creation. Once again, this greater change of identity is reflected in the Passover story.

Growing up I often heard it stated that the covenants of the Old Testament were for the Jews. Then a pastor would turn to the Old Testament and pull out a promise that was made there and apply it to the church. Over time I realized that what they were really saying was that the judgments of the Old Testament covenants were for the Jews, but the promises that were made as part of Old Testament covenants were now intended for the gentile church.

Imagine my surprise when I discovered that the covenants of God in the Old Testament are not limited to one people group. When Abraham was given the sign of circumcision, the sign of a covenant, every member of His household was to be circumcised alongside Abraham. We know for a fact that there was only one person in the entire household who was a blood descendant of Abraham. Everyone else was a foreigner. Eliezer of Damascus was his heir before the birth of Ishmael, and Abraham had 318 fighting men in his household in Genesis 14. All of these men were part of the covenant that was made with Abraham, because they were of the household of Abraham.

We see this again in Passover. When Israel left Egypt there was a "mixed multitude" (Exodus 12:38) that went with them. This mixed multitude included people from nations other than Israel who through the events of the plagues and Passover decided that it was better to go with Israel and serve their God than to stay in Egypt after the collapse. In the Torah and later books we catch a glimpse of at least one of the men who would have been part of this mixed multitude. This man is none other than Caleb, the faithful witness of the land alongside Joshua in Numbers 13-14.

We first read about Caleb in Numbers 13 when he is chosen as the spy that was to represent the tribe of Judah as one of the twelve spies. But if we continue reading about the man Caleb, we find out later that Caleb was not a descendent of Judah! Instead, Caleb was a Kennizzite:

> Surely none of the men who came up out of Egypt, from twenty years old and upward, shall see the land that I swore to give to Abraham, to Isaac, and to Jacob, because they have not wholly followed me, none except Caleb the son of Jephunneh the **Kenizzite** and Joshua the son of Nun, for they have wholly followed the LORD.
> —Numbers 32:11-12

So the question arises, who are the Kenizzites? Where did they come from? Well, to discover this, we need to turn back to Genesis 15 when the LORD made the initial covenant with Abraham that His seed would become a nation:

> On that day the LORD made a covenant with Abram, saying, "To your offspring I give this land, from the river of Egypt to the great river, the river Euphrates, the land of the Kenites, the **Kenizzites**, the Kadmonites, the Hittites, the Perizzites, the Rephaim, the Amorites, the Canaanites, the Girgashites, and the Jebusites."
> —Genesis 15:18-21

Surprise, Surprise! The Kenizzites were a nation that inhabited the land of Canaan that Israel was set to inherit in the upcoming conquest! They were not one of the seven nations that were to be shown no quarter, but they were inhabitants in Canaan nonetheless. They were one of the nations that were to be driven out of the land. It is this man that was chosen to be the representative of Judah as they traveled through the land.

And why not? We can assume that it was likely that Caleb would have been familiar with the local customs and languages. Even if Caleb had been a slave since birth alongside Israel, it is likely that his parents would have taught him his native language. In this role, he likely would have acted as a guide for the other eleven who had probably never been to Canaan prior to this. This is not the surprising fact in this story, though. Instead, the surprising fact for most is that a person from a nation outside of Israel would be included in the number of Judah, and that this person would be rewarded above all of the "native-born" of his generation by being allowed to enter the land during the conquest. All others apart from Joshua and the Levites died in the wilderness. Caleb, this man from the nations and native of Canaan, was grafted in as part of the tribe of Judah. He became a powerful force in the conquest and a primary representative of Judah at the time.

This story demonstrates that long before Paul penned the words of Romans 11, the concept of individuals from the nations being included in the covenants of Israel was always part of God's plan for the world. When we then enter into the covenant of Jesus, we become citizens of the commonwealth of Israel (Ephesians 2:12-13), just as those who took on the sign of circumcision were added to the covenant of Abraham. Just like Caleb and the rest of the mixed multitude who left Egypt alongside the native-born of Israel, those who come under the blood of the lamb are part of Israel. This is why all who were from the nations were to become circumcised before participating in the Passover memorial. This was a sign that they were included in the nation of Israel. They were part of the household of Abraham.

For Christians today, partaking in Passover is not a matter of the flesh. Just as Abraham's faith was counted as righteousness in Genesis 15 before God forged a covenant with him, we who trust in God in faith are the seed of Abraham. We are included in His household, regardless of our nationality, ethnicity, race, language, or culture. All who are the seed of Abraham, according to faith and not a work of the flesh, are then counted as part of Israel.

When redemption occurs in our lives, we identify with the death and resurrection of Jesus as an act of dedication to Him. In that moment our allegiances to this world cease. We become part of a kingdom that is greater than this world—a kingdom of light and life that transcends borders and languages. It is this kingdom that we serve above all others regardless of what our profession or status might be. We take on a new identity in relationship to God over all else. Our faith defines us from then on. Not our nationality. Not our careers. Not our sex or gender. Nothing but our relationship to Messiah. He becomes our alpha and omega. The beginning and the end of our lives. Nothing matters more than Him.

The Fulfillment of Passover

Passover is a truly foundational part of the life of every believer. It depicts every aspect of the process of salvation that each and every one of us has experienced. The revelations in this story have the power to transform our lives and provide fuel for living out our faith in the world. Every aspect of Passover that has been covered up to this point becomes one more facet of our lives. But the Biblical development of

Passover does not stop here. There is much more to Passover as it is revealed in the life of Jesus.

With that in mind, let's examine how the story of Passover is depicted in the Gospels through the life, death, burial, and resurrection of Jesus, our Messiah.

PART 2
PASSOVER AND MESSIAH

When it comes to significant Biblical events such as Passover, we can be sure that there are ways that Jesus fulfilled the event in the course of His life and ministry. Paul says it in Colossians (Col. 2:17). The Sabbaths and Festivals are shadows of our Messiah. Throughout the themes of Passover, we find aspects of the Gospel. The foundations of our relationship to and interaction with God are present in a multitude of ways. By exploring these themes in greater depth, we can confirm that Jesus fulfilled the Passover. But what does it mean that Jesus fulfilled something that was previously written? We see this language used all over the place in the New Testament:

> Do not think that I have come to abolish the Law or the
> Prophets; I have not come to abolish them but to **fulfill** them.
> —Matthew 5:17

> But what God foretold by the mouth of all the prophets, that
> his Christ would suffer, he thus **fulfilled**.
> —Acts 3:18

Often when this idea is understood, there is a cultural push to make this idea of fulfillment mean that these things that were done by Jesus are now complete and so we don't have any obligation to follow through on our own. Matthew 5:17 is an example of this type of application. I have heard it said that Messiah fulfilled the law so that I don't have to. This is an idea that permeates the church to one degree or another. Although the Greek word for fulfill, *pleroo* (πληρόω), can be used in certain contexts to mean finishing something, that is not its only meaning. Rather *pleroo* bears the meaning of "cramming something full," "leveling out a hollow," "satisfying certain conditions," or "finishing a task or period of time."[1]

Think of *pleroo* as a cup that has been filled to the brim with water. The cup has been *pleroo*(ed), its purpose has been fulfilled and the cup has reached the fullest of its potential. The cup is not finished and it certainly does not cease to exist or be applicable. The cup still exists and can become an example of how other cups can have their potential fulfilled in a similar manner. The law in the context of Matthew 5:17 acts the same way. Jesus filled up the cup of the Torah and Prophets and imbued meaning into the words written there. Because of His filling of the cup, we can look at His cup and then strive to fill our cups in the same way.

Jesus truly did fulfill the themes of Passover. In fact, without Jesus and His work, we would not be able to pinpoint the themes of Passover so accurately. The substance truly does help us to make sense of the shadow. But the word pleroo also bears the idea of fulfilling certain conditions. And with a little knowledge of first-century Passover practices, we can find that Jesus also fulfilled the conditions of the Passover sacrifice in His death, burial, and resurrection.

We have seen it before in this book, and the New Testament makes it very clear: Jesus was the Passover lamb for all who believe in Him. Paul comes right out and states this in 1 Corinthians 5. His declaration in this verse is the clearest statement of Jesus's role in the packing-full-of-meaning of Passover. But we must be careful to not impose this particular view everywhere that we think that the idea of fulfillment might fit.

---

1   https://biblehub.com/greek/4137.htm.

So before we go further, let's dispel a common misconception. This particular misconception is so widespread that it is used by anti-missionaries in attempts to discredit the reliability of the New Testament. When we examine this passage in depth, we will discover that this particular claim has nothing to do with Passover. Rather, this particular declaration points to another shadow that our Messiah fulfilled.

The Lamb who Takes away Sin

In John 1, before Jesus appears in the scene, John the Baptist and his ministry are introduced. In John 1:29, as Jesus enters the narrative, John declares the following:

> The next day he saw Jesus coming toward him, and said, "Behold, the Lamb of God, who takes away the sin of the world!
> —John 1:29

This declaration of John is often likened to the declaration of Paul in 1 Corinthians 5 that Jesus is the Passover Lamb. This simply is not the case. The fact is that the Passover lamb did not take away sins. If we claim that this is what John the Baptist was announcing, we provide an unnecessary toehold for those who seek to tear down the validity of the New Testament. Because Passover did not deal with sin, we must admit that John's declaration is not connected to Passover. Rather, this interpretation stems from ignorance of the festivals as outlined in the Torah. You see, there was another festival at another time of year in which the sins of Israel were taken away from Israel: Yom Kippur, the Day of Atonement.

On Yom Kippur, two goats were chosen from the congregation and brought before God. Lots were cast over the goats and one became a sacrifice, while the other goat was taken into the wilderness to carry away the sins of the people:

> And Aaron shall lay both his hands on the head of the live goat, and confess over it all the iniquities of the people of Israel, and all their transgressions, all their sins. And he shall put them on the head of the goat and send it away into the wilderness by the hand of a man who is in readiness. The goat shall bear all their iniquities on itself to a remote area, and he shall let the goat go free in the wilderness.
> —Leviticus 16:21-22

This goat, commonly referred to as the scapegoat, carried the sins of Israel to a place of death and destruction. On the day of Yom Kippur, the removal of the sins of the people was not something that was based on a sacrifice. Rather, the sins or iniquities of Israel were put on the head of the goat, and the goat was led into the wilderness to carry them away.

But wait! Leviticus states that it is a goat, not a lamb, that carries away the sins of the people. So, how does John the Baptist's declaration that Jesus is the lamb who takes away the sins of the world connect to Yom Kippur? Well, let's remember that the word for lamb in the Hebrew language and culture can mean either a goat or a sheep:

> Your lamb shall be without blemish, a male a year old. You may take it from the sheep or from the goats.
> —Exodus 12:5

In the biblical culture, the word "lamb" was used to refer to either sheep or goats. Therefore, it is not a stretch to infer that John the Baptist did not have Passover in mind when speaking of Jesus as the lamb. Rather, John speaks of the lamb in reference to the role Jesus played in the removal of sins from Israel. This removal is itself a fulfillment of the Yom Kippur ritual. Let's not forget that it was after Jesus's baptism by John the Baptist, as recorded in each of the synoptic gospels, that Jesus was led into the wilderness for His 40 days of fasting and trial. Jesus's life in this instance brought a deeper meaning to the Yom Kippur ritual that had been practiced for 1500 years previously. Understanding how John's declaration and Jesus' actions together fulfill this ancient festival gives us a tool to interpret other passages of Scripture. This tool is using our knowledge of the Hebrew Scriptures—the shadows of Messiah as it were—and leveraging this knowledge in our understanding of what New Testament authors say. Using this tool in John 1:29 began with understanding the Yom Kippur ritual. We didn't even need to know the entire ritual, only one small piece that was pertinent to the statement that John the Baptist made. With this past knowledge, we can more accurately interpret the New Testament through the lens of the Old. Doing this allows us to not only be able to use the substance to understand the shadows, but with knowledge of the shadows, we can also better understand the substance. With this in mind, we can apply this same methodology to Passover in relation to the life of Jesus. But to fully understand this, we must also familiarize ourselves with the practice of Passover during the time of Jesus, just as we needed to understand the practice of Yom Kippur in the Torah.

Passover in the Second Temple Era

Contrary to popular opinion, Jews of the first century were not monolithic. They did not agree on how to practice or how to interpret the Torah, and this reality didn't disappear when it came to the observance of Passover. There were many sects of Jewish religious practice in the first century, with the Pharisees and Sadducees being among the smallest but most influential groups. Other religious Jewish sects in the first century included Scribes, Essenes, Herodians, Zealots, and Nazarenes, among a slew of other minor factions that are not specifically mentioned in the Bible and which have been lost to history. Each sect had its own understanding and interpretation of the Torah and its own way of attempting to live the precepts of the Torah in their lives.

It should also be recognized that the temple at the time of Jesus was not being run as it was supposed to. While Levites served in the temple and priests were of the line of Aaron, the High Priest was not a Levite at all. Instead, the High Priest at the time of Jesus was a political appointee, and in the first century, this position was up for auction and could only be afforded by the incredibly wealthy. This ensured that the High Priest was not only wealthy but also pro-Roman. It is mentioned in Luke 3:2 that there was a sort of dual High Priesthood in operation at the time of Jesus. Both Annas and Caiaphas are called High Priests, but when we turn to John 18:13, we find that Annas was the father-in-law of Caiaphas. How could this be?

Early on in the Roman occupation of Israel, beginning with Herod the Great, the Romans took control of the office of the High Priest. Once this occurred, this office never again reverted to the sons of Aaron. In 6 CE Annas was appointed as the first High Priest in the newly formed Roman province of Iudaea (Judea). He served in this office until 15 CE when he was deposed by the Roman procurator Valerius Gratus. After his deposition, Annas retained a great amount of influence and was able to secure the office of High Priest for four of his sons and his son-in-law Ciaphas. Annas was, for all intents and purposes, the man behind the power that was granted to the office of High Priest. For many Jews, once Annas was appointed High Priest, he remained High Priest as this office was supposed to last until death.

Because of this Caiaphas was seen as the public face of the office. This state of affairs is just one easily recognizable point of evidence that the temple was not what it was intended to be.

Add to this that there is ample evidence that, contrary to popular belief, the majority of Passover sacrifices in the centuries surrounding the life of Jesus were not accomplished at the temple. Rather, the majority of Passover sacrifices were done domestically. Now when I say domestically, I am not claiming that these sacrifices were accomplished in the home as was done for the first Passover. Instead, everyone who wished to participate in Passover would travel to Jerusalem and the sacrifices would occur in various areas around the city.

This claim might seem preposterous. After all, we know how the sacrifices were accomplished in the temple because this sacrifice is described in Mishnah Pesachim 5. According to this chapter of the Mishnah, "all of the Pesach sacrifices were accomplished" within the course of reciting the Hillel psalms (Psalms 113-118) three times. In this tractate, the Mishnah claims that there was never a time that the number of worshippers in the temple did not accomplish the sacrifice in the time it takes to make this recitation. Some historians have done the calculations necessary to discover just how many men could fit in the temple courtyard at one time. According to Joachim Jeremias, each course would have been around 6400 men at most due to space limitations for worshipers, lambs, and priests.[2] This places the number of Passover lambs that could have been slain in the temple at 19,200. Josephus, however, records something vastly different in the year 70 CE, the final year that the temple stood:

---

2   Joachim Jeremias, *Jerusalem in the Times of Jesus: An Investigation into Economic and Social Conditions during the New Testament Period* (Philadelphia: Fortress Press, 1969), 79-83.

> So these high priests, upon the coming of that feast which is
> called the Passover, when they slay their sacrifices, from the
> ninth hour till the eleventh, but so that a company not less
> than ten belong to every sacrifice...found the number of sac-
> rifices was two hundred and fifty-six thousand five hundred;
> which, upon the allowance of no more than ten that feast
> together, amounts to two million seven hundred thousand
> and two hundred persons that were holy and pure...
> —Josephus, *Wars of the Jews* 4.9.3

256,500 Pesach sacrifices were accomplished in 70AD. That is a number that is orders of magnitude greater than the 19,200 sacrifices that the record from the Mishnah allows for according to modern calculations. The only viable conclusion is that the vast majority of these sacrifices were accomplished throughout the city, and not specifically at the temple.

But sacrifices were to be made in the Temple! Deuteronomy 16 makes it clear that the Passover sacrifice was to be accomplished in the place God chose. As I mentioned in part 1, the place where God chose to make His Name dwell was not specifically the temple, but rather Jerusalem. Thus, it is easy to see how disagreements in interpretation and practice could arise. After all, not only was the sacrifice to be offered in the place that God chose, the sacrifice was to be cooked and eaten in this same place as well. No serious scholar suggests that the sacrifice was to be eaten in the temple because it is truly impractical.

So let's consider all of these data in conjunction. Considering the fractured state of the Jews, the inability of the temple to handle this vast number of people, and the rise in disagreements on how to interpret various passages, it is easy to see how many Jews in the first century would have concluded that offering the Passover sacrifice domestically was the proper way to sacrifice. Since the first Passover was offered in the homes and there was no specific command changing this practice, then the practice was seen to stand. It was not until the time of Hezekiah that we find the first recorded Passover sacrifice occurring in the temple. In the time of Ezra, we read in chapter 6 of the book that bears his name that the priests would offer a single Passover lamb in the temple on behalf of all Israel. It seems that these late scriptural examples led various sects to the conclusion that all Passover sacrifices were to be slaughtered in the temple, but not everyone agreed.

So, how did Judah get to this place where the temple was being run by puppets that were appointed by a foreign power? How did there arise such a divide over where to sacrifice the Passover lamb? What changed from the time of Ezra and Nehemiah when Judah returned to the land and held their first Passover in decades (Ezra 6:19-21), to the fragmented society that history tells us existed in the time of Jesus? To discover this, we need to look at the period that is commonly known as the "intertestamental period." That is, the approximately 400 years of silence between the book of Malachi and the earliest events of the time of Jesus that are recorded in the book of Luke. This exploration will help to set the stage for the ministry of Jesus and the state of the Holy Land during His ministry.

A Brief History of Second Temple Judea: Babylon

In 597 BCE, King Nebuchadnezzar of Babylon finally conquered Judah and began a process of deporting Judean citizens from Judah to Babylon. This process of deportations lasted around ten years, during which several rebellions arose and were defeated as recorded in the book of Jeremiah. This process of exile culminated in the destruction of the first temple around 586 BCE. During this time, not every Jewish citizen was deported. Rather, the wealthy, important, and powerful were taken from the Jewish homeland and the rest of the citizens were left without leadership or infrastructure. No more central government. No landholders or business owners. By the time the deportations were finished, only peasants and slaves remained in the land, leaving behind a power vacuum that we see hinted at in Jeremiah 40-45. As for the deportations, it is estimated that there were only around 10,000 men (not including women and children) who were initially transported to Babylon.

For the following several decades, the people of Judah faced hardship, either through exile or extreme poverty due to internal conflict and oppression from neighboring nations. Then in 539 BCE, the Babylonian Empire fell to the Persians under the leadership of King Cyrus.

A Brief History of Second Temple Judea: Persia

Only a hundred years before they defeated and supplanted Babylon, the Persians had been little more than shepherds with little power in the world. But in the middle seventh century BCE, a man named Zarathustra began to teach in Persia and founded what would become known as Zoroastrianism. Zoroastrianism is a religion that teaches of two gods, one good and one evil, who battle in the heavens and who will bring the world to a great battle in the last days. The winner of this final conflict would then rule the world for all eternity. Cyrus was brought up in this religion and it was his religious belief that led him to attempt to conquer the world. He believed in that final battle at the end of days and so started a conquest as an attempt to secure as much power as possible for the side of good to ensure that good would win in the end. To this end, Cyrus captured Babylon in a single night, overthrew the king, and became the de facto ruler of the world, although he did not yet control all parts of it.

At some point in the early years of his reign, Cyrus came into contact with a scroll of Isaiah, and he was so impressed that Isaiah called him out by name over 145 years earlier that in 536 BCE, Cyrus commanded the return of the Jewish people to their homeland.[3] It is in Isaiah 45, in this message to Cyrus, the LORD establishes that He is the only God. Cyrus, who saw all foreign gods as belonging to either good or bad, identified the LORD as not just a good God, but as The God from this and so He commanded that the worship of the LORD be reestablished in Judea. The year that the first of the exiles returned to Judah from Persia they built an altar as the first step of restarting the worship of the LORD. Judah, according to Persian decree, was to be reestablished as a theological state as part of the Persian Empire. It was, however, another 20 years before the temple was rebuilt in 515 BCE and full temple worship resumed.

For the next two centuries, Judah existed as a tribute state of Persia enjoying a mostly peaceful existence as vassals of the Persian Empire. During this time, the worship of the LORD was fostered and encouraged by the leadership in Persia. During these centuries of relative peace, the synagogue system was founded in Judah as an additional way to worship outside of the temple.

You see, while Israel had been in Babylon, there were many, in the manner of Daniel, who did not wish to stop worshiping the LORD, and there were many more who realized just how far they had fallen and returned to the worship of the LORD. But there was no temple. And so a form of house church was established, which then evolved into a predecessor of our modern church organization. Communal buildings were set aside as places where people could gather together to worship. When Israel then returned to Judah and the temple was

---

3   Josephus, Antiquities 11.1.1-2.

rebuilt, this system of local places of worship did not simply go away. Instead, the synagogue was born and nearly every community established a place for local communal worship throughout Judah. Now, not only were there priests and Levites who ran the temple and its rituals, there were also people throughout the land who taught about God and His ways. This system gave rise to the rabbis and sages of the second temple period.

A Brief History of Second Temple Judea: Greece

In 336 BCE, a man named Alexander of Macedon became the king of Macedonia when his father Philip II was assassinated at a royal wedding. For the next few years, Alexander began a campaign to reunite the Grecian clans and establish order in Greece. It was in 334 BCE that Alexander then invaded the Persian Empire and began his decade-long conquest of Persia and its territories, including Judah. By 332 BCE, Alexander was the king of Egypt, by 330 BCE he was crowned King of Persia, and in 326 BCE he invaded India. In a matter of twelve years, Alexander conquered the known world and created the largest empire the world had ever known. His reign was short-lived, however, as in 323 BCE, Alexander died in the palace of Nebuchadnezzar II in Babylon at the age of 32.

When Alexander died, Perdiccas was appointed to the throne until he was assassinated two years later in 321 BCE. At this point, the empire that Alexander had formed fell into disarray and his generals initiated a forty-year-long war to determine who would succeed Alexander as leader of the Empire. When stability was finally reached, the empire that had been unified under Alexander was split into four separate hostile empires. The Ptolemaic Empire in the areas of Egypt, the Seleucid Empire covered Mesopotamia and central Asia, the Attalid Kingdom covered most of Asia Minor, and the Antigonid

Empire ruled Greece and Macedonia. In 312 BCE, Judah came under the control of the Seleucid Empire.

One of the greatest effects of the defeat of Persia and the institution of Greek rule was the introduction of Hellenism into Jewish culture. You see, the Persians were happy to have people live within their own unique culture, and even supported the diversity of cultures within their empire. Their Persian Empire was theistic in that the kingdom was founded for religious purposes, but as long as a people or their gods were seen as good according to Zoroastrianism, then the culture of the people was left alone and even fostered. When the Greeks began to conquer the world, their culture followed them, and programs were begun to introduce Hellenism into every culture that they controlled. Greeks viewed their own culture as superior to others and their rule was seen as a way of civilizing barbarian cultures. When the Seleucids came to power in Mesopotamia, in the beginning, the allowance of the Jewish culture and religion was tolerated while Hellenism was praised and practiced widely. These two cultures existed side by side with some friction but were peaceful for the most part. That was until Antiochus IV, also known as Antiochus Epiphanes, came to power in 175 BCE.

A Brief History of Second Temple Judea: Seleucids

There is no clear consensus on what caused the change in Seleucid policy towards the Jews, only that it happened and it happened quickly. The leading thought is that there was a disagreement between the Jews and their Seleucid rulers over the leadership of the temple and the office of High Priest. This disagreement was then exacerbated by a particularly violent and bloody revolt by a Jewish sect that was opposed to the Hellenization of the Jews.[4] The book of 2 Maccabees records that while Antiochus was in Egypt prosecuting a campaign against the Ptolemy Empire, a rumor began to be spread around Judea of his death. This rumor caused Jason, the High Priest who had been deposed by Antiochus, to gather 1,000 troops to storm Jerusalem, causing Menelaus, the High Priest that had been appointed by Antiochus to replace Jason, to flee Jerusalem in the ensuing riots. When the Emperor received the news from Judea, he had recently suffered a defeat in Egypt. And so when he returned to Jerusalem he came in force:

> When news of what had happened reached the king, he took it to mean that Judea was in revolt. So, raging inwardly, he left Egypt and took the city by storm. And he commanded his soldiers to cut down relentlessly everyone they met and to slay those who went into the houses. Then there was the killing of young and old, destruction of boys, women, and children, and slaughter of virgins and infants. Within the total of three days eighty thousand were destroyed, forty thousand in hand-to-hand fighting; and as many were sold into slavery as were slain.
> —2 Maccabees 5:11-14 (RSV)

During the battle, Menelaus took Antiochus to the temple, where he stole all the gold and occupied Jerusalem with 22,000 troops. The institution of this occupying force seemed peaceful at first, and then these soldiers were set free to slaughter on a Sabbath day resulting

---

4   Martin Hengel, *Judaism, and Hellenism: Studies in Their Encounter in Palestine During the Early Hellenistic Period* (Eugene, OR: Wipf and Stock, 1974).

in the deaths of thousands more of the inhabitants of Jerusalem in retribution for the revolt.

This distaste for Jews and their religious practice caused Antiochus to outlaw the Jewish religion and practices to the point of forbidding circumcision, forcing work to be done on the Sabbath, and forbidding the celebration of the holy days. He went so far as to dedicate the Jerusalem temple to Zeus, offering unclean sacrifices and practicing orgies within the temple grounds. Jews were forced under penalty of death to offer sacrifices to pagan gods and to participate in their holidays. Women who were caught with circumcised sons would have their babies killed and hung around their necks before they would be paraded to the city walls and thrown off. Anyone who showed any sign of remaining true to the LORD or His practices was publicly shamed and summarily executed.

Oppression by the Seleucids ultimately resulted in the Maccabean revolt. For seven years, the Maccabees succeeded in driving the Seleucids from Judah and securing a measure of autonomy for Israel. With this autonomy came a return of freedom to worship. This episode of nearly a decade of complete persecution and suppression of religious practices, however, served to splinter the Jewish faith into small close-knit communities that were disconnected from the synagogues. Anyone who desired to retain their faith had to do so in private and so there was little to no communication between these communities. The result was that these small communities began to drift away from each other in teaching and interpretation. Those who attempted to remain true during this time and who were able to remain hidden became isolated from others around them. Judaism was already somewhat fractured before this point, but it was at this time that the religion splintered into multiple sects with a variety of teachers and beliefs.

A Brief History of Second Temple Judea: Hasmoneans

After the Seleucid Empire was driven out of Israel, a power vacuum formed in Judea. At the time of the Maccabean victory, only two of the five Hasmonean sons (the leaders of the rebellion who were called the Maccabees as a nickname) survived: Jonathan and Simon. Just because they had been defeated did not mean that the Seleucids had given up their desire to rule Judah. Instead, their attempts became more subversive as assassination plots and attempts at pitting Jews against each other were carried out throughout the land.

Shortly after the defeat of the Seleucid Empire, Jonathan was appointed as High Priest, but even though he was pressured, he did not claim the office of king over Judea. During his tenure as High Priest, Jonathan was captured by Seleucid sympathizers who turned him over to the Seleucids who held him for ransom. The ransom demands included the relinquishing of control of certain cities and allowing Seleucid forces to re-enter Jerusalem. These demands were refused and Jonathan was publicly executed in response leaving Simon as the last remaining Hasmonean.

In 141 BCE Simon established the Hasmonean dynasty as its king with overwhelming popular support, and he was appointed as High Priest. Judea became a semi-autonomous state under his rule that primarily functioned on its own, but still paid taxes to the Seleucids. Over the next several decades the Seleucid empire weakened under near-constant attack from the Parthians and Romans until Judea was able to secure near-complete autonomy in 110 BCE.

Once Judea was free from Seleucid control they began to expand outward capturing the areas of Samaria, Galilee, Iturea, Perea, and Idumea under Hasmonean control. For the next fifty years, Judea was free of any outside control. During this time the king and High Priest attempted to consolidate the worship practices of Israel. It was also during this time that the political parties of the Pharisees and Sadducees made their first appearance. The Pharisees pushed against many of the decisions made by some of the later Hasmonean kings, but it was their protest of the offices of king and High Priest being held by one man that finally drove a rift between these two sects. In response to this protest of the Pharisees, Alexander Jannaeus openly sided with the Sadducees going so far as to adopt their rites into the temple. This caused a brief civil war in Judea which ended with the bloody suppression of the Pharisees.

Alexander's widow Salome Alexandra succeeded him to the throne upon his death and it was she that raised the Pharisees back into influence by her recognition and legitimization of the Pharisee led Sanhedrin. This division in the religious system that was so closely tied to the political system again led to another civil war not long after. This war was fought between the sons of Alexander and Salome. Hyrcanus was supported by the Pharisees, and Aristobulus was supported by the Sadducees, and this war only concluded when Jerusalem was conquered by Roman general Pompey in 63 BCE.

It was during this time that the first records were made of practices and traditions that were seen as authoritative. The collection of writings that would later be codified as the Mishnah was begun, but attempts to codify the religious practices were not without competition.

From the time of the defeat of the Seleucid Empire at the hands of the Maccabees, the Ptolemaic Empire sought to gain influence in Judea. One of the ways that this was accomplished was by the introduction of Egyptian influences into the fractured believing communities. Because there was to be no attempt at consolidation of the faith for several decades yet, these influences found some fertile ground. Now, in addition to Hellenistic influences, there were Egyptian influences to contend with, as well as the lingering Babylonian and Persian influences brought back from captivity. Even more, when the Greeks turned the temple system into a puppet of the state, many Jews began to distrust what was being taught by the temple, and so various teachers began to gather students to themselves and set themselves up as the "true" teachers of the Torah. It was from these teachers that the practice of baptism was formalized. Any attempts to unify Judaism at this point were powerless in the face of history, politics, and human nature.

A Brief History of Second Temple Judea: Romans

When Pompey captured Rome in 63 BCE, Rome did not immediately depose the Hasmonean dynasty. Instead, Judea became a Roman protectorate with a Judean king on the throne. Hyrcanus II served as ethnarch, a Greek term for the ruler of an ethnic group or kingdom, as well as High Priest. The real power in Judea was Antipater, an Edomite, and the father of Herod the Great. This separation of power between Rome and the Hasmoneans continued for another 26 years until Herod the Great was appointed king of Judea by Rome, thus ending the reign of the Hasmonean dynasty in Judea.

From this point on, the Herodian dynasty ruled Judea as a Roman protectorate until 6 CE when Emperor Augustus deposed Herod Archelaus and took direct control of the rulership of all Judean provinces, giving Rome the authority to punish by execution for the first time. After this point, the Herodian dynasty continued until 92 CE, but their position and power were greatly diminished as vassals under Roman control.

A Brief History of Second Temple Judea: Jewish Sects

This history provides the background that sets the stage for the claim that I made earlier. That is, Judaism of the first century was not as monolithic as we commonly conceptualize it. Many influences and teachings were grasping for the attention of the common man, and the primary opponents of Jesus were not necessarily the most prominent viewpoints. They did, however, represent the most vocal, powerful, and influential viewpoints of the day. So let's examine the most prominent sects of Judaism in the first century.

The Sadducees controlled the temple and were open to Helleniza- tion. They became political puppets who were often used to support Roman edicts and provide legitimacy to Roman policies to the people. The Sadducees tended to be aristocratic and they were strict literalists when it came to Biblical interpretation. Hence the aside in Mark 12:18 points out that the Sadducees did not believe in the resurrection.

The Pharisees controlled the synagogues and the Sanhedrin (The Jewish courts). They resisted Hellenization and believed that the temple purity laws applied to all men, whether in the temple or not. It was this attempt to resist Hellenization that led to the creation of "fences" that were placed around the Torah in the form of the impo- sition of oral traditions on the people as commandments. The thing that might be surprising to most is that Josephus records that there were only around 6,000 strict Pharisees in Judea (*Antiquities* 17.2.4), and it is thought that the Pharisees outnumbered the Sadducees!

The scribes were a highly influential group that is thought to have been founded by Ezra. They controlled the text and implementation of the Torah when applicable in legal cases. This sect was the most educated of the Jewish sects of the first century, and by the time of Jesus they had organized various schools throughout Judah, and it is from the scribes that many of the Rabbis of the first century received their education.

The Essenes were another influential sect, even though they were a much smaller community than either the Sadducees or the Pharisees. The Essenes practiced extreme asceticism (denial of sensual pleasure) and it is these traditions which are called "works of the law," in the Dead Sea scrolls 4QMMT, a doctrine that Paul taught against in the books of Romans and Galatians. Josephus records that the Essenes "seem to have a greater affection for one another than other sects have," as the Essenes lived in close-knit closed communities that only welcomed others who were willing to submit to their brand of religious thought.

The Zealots were a religious band that became politically focused seeking to establish a fully autonomous Jewish state. They were highly nationalistic and sought to incite the people of Judah into rebellion against the Roman occupiers. In Antiquities 18.1.6, Josephus records that the Zealots agreed with the Pharisees in interpretation of the Torah, but not in application. While Pharisees were more peaceful, attempting to live peaceably amid oppression, the Zealots became obsessed with the idea of freedom and autonomy from all foreign rule.

A splinter group of Zealots known as the Sicarii had the same general goals as the Zealots, but were more extreme in the execution of their goals. While the Zealots sought to form groups of rebels to fight against Roman occupation in the manner of the Maccabees, the Sicarii acted more like assassins. They would walk through crowds with daggers hidden in their cloaks and would attack Romans and Roman sympathizers and then disappear into the crowd. There are even recorded instances of Sicarii killing devout Jews in an attempt to blame the Romans for the deaths and cause the populace to rise up against Rome.

The Herodians were a fully Hellenized sect of Jews that were friendly with King Herod. They saw Greek influence and culture as the way of progress for Judaism and the Jewish people. They too sought an autonomous Jewish state, only they wanted this state to be formed under a Herodian dynasty. It is thought by some scholars that many Herodians viewed Herod, or his successors, as the Messiah who would eventually overthrow the Roman occupation and free Judah from their influence.

While these are just the most popular of the religious sects in the first century because they are attested to in the New Testament and Historical sources, these were not all that there were. The Pharisees, of which there were around 6,000 practitioners, were the largest. If there were, as Josephus recorded, over 250,000 Passover sacrifices, or 2.5 to 3 million religious Jews, then all of these groups added together do not make up even a quarter of practicing Jews in the world at that time. Alongside this were the non-religious (non-Jewish religion) Jews.; those who supported Hellenization and the Roman occupation, or who simply worshiped other gods.

With all of this history, it is no wonder that there was no agreement among Jews on the place of the sacrifice of the Passover lamb, whether temple-based or domestic. Judaism was fractured into a multitude of sects and practices. And the disagreements just in matters of the Passover sacrifice didn't stop there. Evidence suggests that there were disagreements on just how far outside of Jerusalem was too far when it came to the sacrifice, and when the Passover lamb was to be sacrificed! For some sects, the sacrifice occurred at the beginning of the 14th day, just after sundown, but the memorial meal was not eaten until the beginning of the 15th, just after sundown the next day. This means that a whole 24-hour period would pass between the sacrifice and the meal. Other sects, including the priests, would sacrifice on the afternoon of the 14th, after the evening sacrifice, and then eat the meal at the beginning of the 15th, just after sundown. This practice left just a few hours between the sacrifice and the meal. When it came to the practice of Passover, there were as many opinions as there were sects, so digging into specifics can be a bit daunting.

Although not all of these groups are specifically mentioned in the New Testament, they were all part of the first-century Jewish context in which Jesus lived and taught. There truly was a diversity of thought and application of just how the Torah was to be obeyed and how Passover was to be practiced. For this book, however, we will be focusing on specifics of Temple worship in the second temple period, and primarily the practices of the Pharisees and the Sadducees.

Some of the events of the final week, however, were purely traditional exercises or cultural expressions. As we go forward, we will be examining this mix as it pertains to the topic at hand. We will find that many cultural traditions, temple practices, and teachings of the two primary sects that Jesus interacted with were included in the written accounts of Jesus. But the primary focus is going to be on the events that Jesus fulfilled as the Passover lamb which was done in accordance with the temple service of the day and the written word of the Torah.

As one last caveat, we must recognize that the accounts of Jesus's life as recorded in the gospels were not created to be a history lesson. Each author had a theme that they wished to highlight in their work and so the things that each author records, and even the order in which episodes of Jesus's life are told, are all leveraged towards highlighting the theme that the author was attempting to portray. The fallout of this is that there are disagreements between the authors on the timing and order of events, specifics of what happened, and records of what was said and who was present at each event. This means that when someone approaches the text in an attempt to discern these things, they will invariably encounter places where they will need to choose one text and author over another.

This has been an issue in Biblical scholarship for years, and it can best be explained by the simple fact that human memory is fallible. What we read is what we should expect when comparing eyewitness accounts. With this in mind, when I approached the text in this exercise, I attempted to treat each of the authors with honor. I have attempted to reconcile all of these accounts and minimize the remaining discrepancies. This does not mean that these instances of seeming disagreement will disappear. Rather, I will do my best to recognize these disagreements and discuss their merits rather than simply excuse them away.

Traveling Towards Jerusalem

Near the end of Jesus's ministry, He makes no secret that He will be killed at some point. This declaration precipitates some of the greatest conflicts between Jesus and His closest disciples. All three of the synoptic gospels record three instances of Jesus making this sort of prediction leading up to His entry into Jerusalem. For each of the three predictions, I will quote from a different synoptic gospel to prove a point. Each time that Jesus spoke of His upcoming death, he mentioned one fact. He will be in the grave for three days.

The first prediction of His death came just after Jesus had fed a multitude of people. The first instance of this prophecy is recorded in Matthew 16:21–23, Mark 8:31–32, and Luke 9:21–22. The event as recorded in Matthew and Mark is likely the most well-known because it was at this point that Jesus rebuked Peter and called him Satan:

> From that time Jesus began to show his disciples that he must
> go to Jerusalem and suffer many things from the elders and

chief priests and scribes, and be killed, and on the third day
be raised. And Peter took him aside and began to rebuke him,
saying, "Far be it from you, Lord! This shall never happen to
you." But he turned and said to Peter, "Get behind me, Satan!
You are a hindrance to me. For you are not setting your mind
on the things of God, but on the things of man."
—Matthew 16:21-23

The second occurrence of Jesus foretelling His death occurs shortly
after the transfiguration in all three Synoptics: Matthew 17:22–23,
Mark 9:30–32, and Luke 9:43–45. It is at this telling that the disciples
remain silent in the face of this news. Matthew records a depression
settling over the disciples, while Luke and Mark state that the disciples
simply did not understand what Jesus was telling them, and out of
some sort of fear they did not question Him any further:

They went on from there and passed through Galilee. And
he did not want anyone to know, for he was teaching his
disciples, saying to them, "The Son of Man is going to be
delivered into the hands of men, and they will kill him. And
when he is killed, **after three days he will rise**." But they did
not understand the saying and were afraid to ask him.
—Mark 9:30-32

Finally, while on the road to Jerusalem, Jesus predicts his death one
last time in Matthew 20:17–19, Mark 10:32–34, and Luke 18:31–34:

And taking the twelve, he said to them, "See, we are going
up to Jerusalem, and everything that is written about the Son
of Man by the prophets will be accomplished. For he will

be delivered over to the Gentiles and will be mocked and shamefully treated and spit upon. And after flogging him, they will kill him, **and on the third day he will rise**." But they understood none of these things. This saying was hidden from them, and they did not grasp what was said.

—Luke 18:31-34

Again, the disciples did not grasp what was being said to them as they approached Jerusalem. This time, their lack of questioning was not due to fear but rather to general confusion, possibly due to some spiritual intervention or their own expectations of what Jesus would achieve.

In the book of John, however, Jesus also speaks of His death on several occasions but not as clearly. The majority of his statements are simply made in passing or hinted at (e.g., John 12:7–8; 13:33). You also have this cryptic statement:

"These things I have spoken to you while I am still with you. But the Helper, the Holy Spirit, whom the Father will send in my name, he will teach you all things and bring to your remembrance all that I have said to you. Peace I leave with you; my peace I give to you. Not as the world gives do I give to you. Let not your hearts be troubled, neither let them be afraid. You heard me say to you, 'I am going away, and I will come to you.' If you loved me, you would have rejoiced, because I am going to the Father, for the Father is greater than I. And now I have told you before it takes place, so that when it does take place you may believe."

—John 14:25-29

In each of these instances in all four gospels, Jesus speaks of His upcoming death. And in most of the records of these statements, He is sure to highlight that there will be three days between His death and resurrection. But these declarations of Jesus near the end of His ministry were not the first hint at His eventual death.

In Matthew 12, Jesus is being pestered by the scribes and Pharisees to provide a sign of His Messiahship. Earlier in the chapter, He had healed a man with a withered hand in a synagogue on the Sabbath, and then a demon-possessed man was brought to Him to be healed. In both situations, Jesus was faced with pushback from the religious leaders who were skeptical of who He was. And so the scribes and Pharisees ask for Jesus to provide a sign to them that He was who He said that He was, and Jesus responds to their request:

> But he answered them, "An evil and adulterous generation seeks for a sign, but no sign will be given to it except the sign of the prophet Jonah. For just as Jonah was three days and three nights in the belly of the great fish, **so will the Son of Man be three days and three nights in the heart of the earth**.
> —Matthew 12:39-40

Once again, the reference to "three days" is included, but this time there is an additional element added to the sign: three nights in the heart of the earth. Now it is no secret that Christian tradition places the death of Jesus on a Friday and His resurrection on Sunday, and if this is the case, then there are at least three partial days in this time-line. But with this view, there is no possible way that you can arrive at "three nights in the heart of the earth."

Christian tradition states that Jesus was crucified on a Friday. With this tradition, it is possible to arrive at three partial days, but there are only two nights at best. Perhaps Jesus was simply using a figure of speech. Justin Martyr, a second century Christian apologist and philosopher, writes the following:

> For He was crucified on the day before that of Saturn; and on the day after that of Saturn, which is the day of the Sun, having appeared to His apostles and disciples, He taught them these things, which we have submitted to you also for your consideration.
>
> —Justin Martyr, *First Apology* 67

This widely recognized early church father states that Jesus was crucified on Friday. Why would we question this conclusion? The answer is because there are some pieces of evidence that are found throughout the gospels that do not fit this view, beginning with (but not limited to) the words of Jesus in Matthew 12:30.

Seeing that this is the case, perhaps we should reexamine the tradition. We could try to create a timeline of Jesus' final week by going through the events described in the gospels and comparing and contrasting the accounts. This may help us to better understand the events and reconcile any discrepancies in the text. By creating this timeline, we may discover that Jesus indeed fulfilled the Passover in a deeper and more significant way. In the end we may find that we arrive at the same conclusion as Church tradition. Even if that is the case, going through the text in this way will sharpen our understanding of Scripture and the role that Jesus played as our Passover sacrifice.

In Preparation for Passover

To better understand the Bible, it can be helpful to consider the cultural context in which the authors lived and wrote. This can provide insight into their perspectives and the intended audience for their writing. Often these topics are not doctrinal or even spiritual; they are simply the way things were done in the past. So, we need to know them before we can truly understand what is being described in the text of the Bible. The authors of the Bible wrote with the assumption that their immediate audience would already be familiar with certain cultural and contextual information, so they did not need to explicitly state it in their writing. Let's explore two of these conventions that we find occurring in the first century, but which are not clear to modern audiences.

Passover or Unleavened Bread

During the first century, the term "Unleavened Bread" referred to the entire eight-day period that included both Passover (one day) and Unleavened Bread (seven days). Josephus states that Unleavened Bread was kept for eight days (*Antiquities* 2.15.1). So we see in first-century literature, the names of the two back-to-back festivals, Unleavened Bread (a seven-day festival) and Passover (one day), began to be used interchangeably, even though technically they are two separate festivals. We find references to this fact in a couple of places in the gospels. Here is just one:

> Now the Feast of Unleavened Bread drew near, which is called the Passover.
> —Luke 22:1

The Festival of Matza is called Passover. The entire eight days are referred to by the name of the first day that is technically separate. But in Josephus, the name "Unleavened Bread" was used to describe both festivals. Recognition of this interchangeable usage of these terms can lead to even further confusion when it comes to attempting to determine a timeline for the final week. If we know what we are looking for, however, we will find that while the names of the festivals are used interchangeably, there are clues scattered throughout the text that can help us to determine the specific timeframe of what is happening in the narrative. However, please understand that what follows is not an exact science. We must make inferences based on what is specifically stated in the text to reach any conclusions. And this is true for anyone who engages in attempting to nail down a timeline for the final week of Jesus. There is no certainty in this practice; there are only levels of probability.

Days and Dates

One last final bit of housekeeping before moving on. This issue arises when discussing the differences between the Hebrew and modern ways of reckoning days. It is a common challenge in these discussions. In the modern west, the day ends and begins at midnight. In other contexts, the day begins at sunrise, or when a person wakes up from their sleep cycle. For the Hebrews and Jews of the first century, however, the day began and ended at sunset. There was no hard line as to when one day ends and another begins. By the first century, because of the potential confusion that this loose overlap between days could produce, the new day was said to have started when three stars could be seen in the night sky. Because Jews of the first century used this way of reckoning time, and the authors of the New Testament spoke of days in this way as well, I will be using this way of accounting time from here on. Throughout the rest of the book, when I state that an event happened at the end of the day, this means that this event occurred before sundown. When an event occurs at the beginning of the day, this event would occur after sundown but before sleep. This may seem a bit confusing or even counterintuitive at first, but establishing this convention will become extremely helpful in the upcoming discussion. So with that, let's use what we have already discovered in part 1 and see what we discover about Jesus' final week.

The Selection of the Lamb

When it comes to the celebration of Passover, the first thing that was to be accomplished was the selection of the sacrificial lamb. We know from Exodus 12 that this was to occur on the tenth day of the month. Unfortunately, the gospels don't come right out and tell us the date of each of the events of Jesus's final week, so if we are going to engage in this process we need to find a place to begin our timeline. Fortunately, the Gospel of John gives us a starting place in relation to Passover where we can begin to collect clues and build a picture of what happened:

> Six days before the Passover, Jesus, therefore, came to Bethany, where Lazarus was, whom Jesus had raised from the dead.
> —John 12:1

"Six days before the Passover." With this we can pin this date of Jesus' arrival at Bethany down to the 8th of the month. He arrived and had dinner at the house of Martha and Lazarus. At this dinner, Mary, the sister of Lazarus, anointed Jesus' feet with oil, an act which

Jesus declares to be in preparation for His own impending burial. The next day, crowds learned that He was in Bethany, so large crowds made their way to Bethany to see Him and Lazarus together, and the priests conspired to kill them. The day after this, Jesus made His way to Jerusalem for the "Triumphal Entry." If this understanding of the timing is right, then the day of the Triumphal entry occurred on the tenth day of the month! That is, the day that the Passover lamb was to be selected by each family.

In the first century, it had become a tradition for the temple to select a single lamb as the representative lamb for the entire nation. This tradition was based on the practice that seems to have been started in the time of Ezra (Ezra 6:19-20). On this day, the High Priest would go out to the temple flocks in Bethlehem to retrieve the lamb that had previously been chosen and set aside for this purpose. What followed was a procession of celebration as the lamb would be led by the High Priest into the city, around to the east side where they would enter through the East Gate, the gate closest to the temple district in Jerusalem. At the entrance of the East Gate, a crowd would form to welcome the lamb as it was led into the city and to the temple. The crowds would shout Hosanna (Save us now) as part of joyous praise and recitation of the Hallel Psalms. In this year, in addition to the entire city greeting the priest with the lamb as he entered the city through the East Gate, the High Priest and Lamb, Jesus, was greeted at the East Gate to the acclaim of the people.

In each of the gospels, we get an account of this event (Matthew 21:1-10; Mark 11:1-11; Luke 19:28-44; John 12:12-16), and in their accounts, each author highlights something slightly different. Each one, however, records the proclamations of "Hosanna" and "blessed is He who comes in the name of the LORD." Growing up, I was taught that these shouts were spontaneous outbursts directed at Jesus specifically. John 12:12 states that large crowds gathered because they had heard that Jesus was coming to Jerusalem. But when we dig into the pageantry of the Passover celebration as described in the Mishnah, we discover that these shouts were not spontaneous, but were rather a communal recitation of Psalm 118—a psalm that is part of the collection of Psalms called the Hallel Psalms (Psalm 113-118), which are a centerpiece of the Passover celebration.

> Save us (Hosanna), we pray, O LORD! O LORD, we pray,
> give us success! Blessed is he who comes in the name of the
> LORD! We bless you from the house of the LORD.
> —Psalm 118:25-26

Accompanying this recitation of the Psalms were also spontaneous shouts declaring Jesus as the Son of David and King of Israel. The account in Matthew emphasizes that a large crowd had assembled to witness a procession, but they were not expecting the procession to involve a king riding on a donkey. Rather the people had gathered to welcome and witness the Passover lamb being led into the city by the High Priest:

> And when he entered Jerusalem, the whole city was stirred up,
> saying, "Who is this?"
> —Matthew 21:11

We expected the High Priest and the Passover lamb, but instead, there is just this man. Who is He? Matthew implies that this Jesus himself is the High Priest and the Lamb. Jesus is the King and Messiah.

The Lamb on Display

On the tenth day, the lamb would be brought into the city by the priest and taken to the temple where it would be displayed for all to see. For the next four days, anyone who had access to the temple and a desire to do so, could come and inspect the lamb to ensure that it was indeed perfect.

When we compare the synoptic gospels' account of the days between the triumphal entry and the crucifixion, we find that this is where Jesus heads directly. As soon as He entered the city of Jerusalem, He went to the temple. In Matthew and Luke, Jesus goes there and immediately cleanses the Temple, but in the Gospel of Mark, when He arrives it is too late, so Jesus goes back to Bethany for the night and returns the next day for the cleansing. The book of John, however, places this incident much earlier in chapter 2 as part of developing a connected theme earlier in the book. Of all of the Gospels, John seems to be the least concerned with the timing of events, even though John is the only gospel that gives us a good starting point to determine the timing of Jesus' final week. The book of John is much more focused on developing certain themes in a certain order, rather than certain events in a certain order.

For the next several chapters, after the triumphal entry, every gospel contains a series of narratives in which Jesus is questioned on the temple grounds. Matthew 22 and Mark 12 recount three instances of each of the major temple based sects questioning Jesus to trap Him. In Luke, the parties are slightly different but the questions and responses are the same.

In Mark 12:13, it is the Pharisees and Herodians who ask Jesus about paying taxes to Caesar. In verse 18, it is the Sadducees who question Jesus about a proverbial woman who had been widowed seven times and then question whose wife she would be in the resurrection—the resurrection that the Sadducees didn't even believe would ever happen. In verse 29, one of the scribes approaches Jesus to ask about the greatest command of the Torah. In verse 35, He then teaches in the temple and in His teaching He turns the tables on these other sects by asking them a trick question about the Messiah. And the chapter finishes with Jesus warning against the scribes (In Matthew 23 it is the Scribes and Pharisees) calling them hypocrites who seek only to make themselves look righteous. Jesus then contrasts their actions by pointing to a widow who gave her last mites to the temple in an act of true righteousness.

Despite causing a disturbance by tossing out the money changers and vendors in the temple, being asked numerous questions by various religious sects and leaders, and openly teaching about the Kingdom of God and criticizing the wealthy while honoring the poor, no one was able to find any fault in Jesus during the short time he spent in the temple. At the end of these few days—one at least and three at most—the desire to kill Jesus grew to the point of action. If they could not find fault with Him, they would simply do away with Him. But through it all, the lamb was inspected and was found to be perfect.

Cleansing the House

In preparation for Passover, there is one more item that was accomplished yearly in every household among practicing Jews in Israel. Every household spent time going through their homes and places of business and discarding any items that were found that contained anything leavened. As previously mentioned, Paul compares leaven to sin that can spread within a community or to the pride that causes some individuals to think more highly of themselves than others. Jesus' criticism of the prideful actions of the scribes during the final week of Passover is particularly fitting given the theme of the holiday:

> And in the hearing of all the people he said to his disciples, "Beware of the scribes, who like to walk around in long robes, and love greetings in the marketplaces and the best seats in the synagogues and the places of honor at feasts, who devour widows' houses and for a pretense make long prayers. They will receive the greater condemnation."
>
> —Luke 20:45-46

In addition to condemning the leaven of the Pharisees, Jesus took other actions during this time that aligned with the command to remove leaven from the home. As mentioned earlier, Jesus purged the temple of the leaven that he found there. Remember, the office of High Priest was occupied at this time by the highest bidder and puppet of Rome, Caiaphas. Due to this, parts of the temple service had become a business designed to make a few rich by exploiting the commands in relation to the common worshiper. The temple had its own coinage, so money changers were needed to exchange other currencies into the temple-approved currency. The transaction would cost, of course, and various services were also offered for a price. In need of an animal for sacrifice? Well, one could be purchased on the temple grounds for a small fee. Vendors and bankers began to profit on the backs of people who had come to worship.

In 1 Corinthians 5:11, as he discusses Passover and the concept of spiritual leaven, Paul identifies individuals who are greedy and fraudulent as part of the group that should be excluded from the community. In this action of driving the money-changers and vendors out of the temple, Jesus is accomplishing this thing that Paul speaks of decades later in connection with Passover. He is cleansing the spiritual leavening out of the house of God, the temple. Jesus' actions highlight the spiritual significance of removing leaven from the home in preparation for Passover, an idea that Paul later expands upon.

Last Supper or Passover Memorial

As Jesus' last day began, He and His disciples retired together to share one final meal. But when you enter into Biblical study on Passover, one thing that you will discover is that there is a lot of debate over the nature of this meal. There is debate among scholars, and even among friends in casual conversation, about whether the final meal shared by Jesus and his disciples was a Passover Memorial meal or if it was simply the last meal Jesus ate before his death. While I don't believe that I am going to solve this dilemma in this work, I am going to throw my opinion into this raging debate. You don't have to agree with me on this, but when it comes to Jesus fulfilling Passover, this view is the most meaningful and satisfies the text the most reliably in my opinion.

So, why is it that this debate rages? There is a debate because the gospels are not clear as to what day this meal occurred. For example, the synoptic gospels each state something along the lines of what we find recorded in Matthew:

> Now on the first day of Unleavened Bread the disciples came
> to Jesus, saying, "Where will you have us prepare for you to
> eat the Passover?"
> —Matthew 26:17

This seems like a clear indication that the meal that Jesus ate with His disciples was in fact a Passover Memorial meal, or in modern language, a Seder. But there may be more going on here than meets the eye because, in the Gospel of John, we read this:

> Some thought that, because Judas had the moneybag, Jesus was telling him, "Buy what we need for the feast," or that he should give something to the poor.
> —John 13:29

Why would the other disciples suspect that Judas was going to buy something for the feast if they were currently eating the feast?

> Then they led Jesus from the house of Caiaphas to the governor's headquarters. It was early morning. They themselves did not enter the governor's headquarters, so that they would not be defiled, but could eat the Passover.
> —John 13:29

The High Priest did not enter Pilate's quarters so that He would not be defiled before Passover.

> Now it was the day of Preparation of the Passover. It was about the sixth hour. He said to the Jews, "Behold your King!"
> —John 19:14

So let's put this all together. Everyone ate the Passover feast at the beginning of the 15th day, after sunset, regardless of when they slaughtered the lamb. The 15th is the first day of the festival of Matza, and as such, it was a day when no one was to engage in any work. Where would Judas find something to purchase for the feast if no one was working? If this was a Seder, did Judas interrupt the officers of the High Priest and the Pharisees that conspired against Jesus while they were having their own Passover Seder? Did they go so far as to risk a city-wide riot in order to crucify Jesus on the High Sabbath of the first day of Matzah? While the Synoptics seem to describe this meal as a memorial, are there other clues in these books that might change this plain reading?

Personally, I find it difficult to believe that the leaders of the Jewish people, who were concerned with their reputation and maintaining purity, would risk their image in front of the public. John makes clear their ritual purity was a big issue in John 18:28. Would this purity-obsessed people risk this purity and the sanctity of the first day of Matzah by engaging in the many trials that were necessary to finally get Roman complicity in His crucifixion on a High Holy Day? I suppose it is possible, but knowing what we know of the Pharisees and their obsession with public image and purity, I find it unlikely.

So the question to be addressed is this: was the final meal of Jesus a Passover Seder or something else? And the fallout of this question will determine whether the trial and crucifixion of Jesus occurred on Passover or on the first day of Matza. Once we can determine this, then the rest will fall into place.

The synoptic gospels seem to all indicate that the last supper was a Passover memorial meal. The gospel of Matthew seems to be stating this clearly, just like the other synoptics:

> Now on the first day of Unleavened Bread the disciples came to Jesus, saying, "Where will you have us prepare for you to eat the Passover?"
> —Matthew 26:17

There it is! It was the first day of Unleavened Bread. We can understand this to mean the day of Passover when the sacrifices occurred if we recognize that these terms are used interchangeably. So that means that the day of the crucifixion would be the first day of the festival of Matzah as stated before—a High Sabbath. But as we continue to read through Matthew, we find something confusing:

> The next day, that is, after the day of Preparation, the chief priests and the Pharisees gathered before Pilate.
> —Matthew 27:62

In Matthew 26:17, the day before the Last Supper was called the first day of Unleavened Bread. But as we continue on, in Matthew 27:62, we find that the day after the crucifixion was the day after the preparation. Preparation of what though? This term, "preparation day" or "day of preparation," is very often used to describe the day before the Sabbath, but this word is also used to describe the day of Passover in John 19:14, 31, & 42. Perhaps we can understand this term in this way in the other gospels such as Matthew? If this is the case, then the crucifixion occurred on Passover day, the day that the lambs were sacrificed and prepared for the memorial later that night. The day before a Sabbath of any sort is called the preparation day, and the first day of Matza is called a High Sabbath. If we believe that Jesus was crucified on the first day of Matzah then we also have to believe that this day was also called the preparation day. So if we view it in this way, then in Matthew 27, the chief priests went to Pilate on the day after the preparation of Passover (the first day of Matza) and asked for guards to be posted at the tomb. The only other option is that this is truly speaking of Saturday, which means that the chief priests and Pharisees gathered before Pilate on the Sabbath to make this request.

In the book of Luke, we see the same thing. In Luke 22:7-13 it seems pretty clear that the Last Supper was meant to be a Passover Memorial. Verse 7 states that it was the day of Unleavened Bread on which the lamb had to be sacrificed. In Verse 8, Jesus tells His disciples to go prepare Passover. Verse 13 states that the disciples prepared Passover once they had found the room that Jesus had described. On the surface, it seems pretty clear. But then in chapter 23, we read something that throws water on this thought:

> It was the day of Preparation, and the Sabbath was beginning.
> —Luke 23:54

This verse states that the day of the crucifixion was the day of Preparation! But the first day of Matza, as a High Sabbath, cannot be a day of preparation, even if it happens on a Friday. It is a day of no work and was treated the same as a Sabbath. Passover day, however, is a day of Preparation for Unleavened Bread, and if it occurs on a Friday it serves as a day of preparation for the Sabbath as well. Mark features this same language:

> And when evening had come, since it was the day of Preparation, that is, the day before the Sabbath.
> —Mark 15:42

Even though Mark also states that it was the day of Passover when the lambs were being sacrificed that the Last Supper occurred (Mark 14:12), Mark 15:42 clearly states—just as in all of the Synoptics—that the day of the crucifixion was the day of preparation and the next day was the Sabbath. It is these three occurrences that have led to the thought that Jesus was crucified on a Friday, but as I have already stated and as I will go into more detail soon, this reference to the day of preparation may just be speaking of Passover day itself, and not the usual weekly Sabbath. And the reference to the Sabbath would then be a reference to the High Sabbath rather than the weekly Sabbath. Viewing it in this way solves some other issues in the text, including the third day and another issue that I will cover soon.

Let's get back to the question at hand. What was the nature of this dinner? The gospels do not seem to agree, which is what leads to this question in the first place. So, let's look to one more source to see if we can find any hints of what might be happening here: Jewish tradition. There are two practices in Judaism, which are pertinent to this discussion that can be traced back to the Mishnah. The first is an event that is called *seudah maphsehket*, loosely translated as "last supper" or "final meal." This meal is something that happens in Judaism before any recognized fast. Today, this practice is primarily associated with the fast of Yom Kippur.

The second event is a specifically Galilean tradition from the first century that was adopted by much of modern Judaism. This event is the fast of the firstborn. This fast was something that was practiced by the firstborn of some Galilean families on the day of Passover (the 14th) in preparation for eating the Passover meal the following night (The beginning of the 15th). This practice was instituted as a way for the firstborn to internalize that it was their lives that had been on the line at the first Passover. It was their lives specifically that had been bought by the blood of the lamb. The fast of the firstborn during the day of Passover was a practice that was limited to worshipers from Galilee in the first century, however, and did not extend into Judea. The *seudah maphsehket* was a widely recognized practice even in Judea when there was a fast at that time.

Add to this that the Mishnah also records in *Pesachim* 4 that, in Judea, work was allowed to be done up until midday on the 14th. However, in the Galilee, no work was allowed on the 14th at all due to custom. This means that, as Galileans, Jesus and His disciples would have finished all preparations for their Passover Memorial on the 13th, the day before Passover officially began. They would not have been finding and securing the room on Passover day. Once they were done with preparations for Passover, they would have then had a final meal together as the beginning of a fast that some of them, including Jesus, would likely have eaten as the 14th started. This fast would then conclude with Passover Memorial the following night, the 15th. This practice from the Galilee in the first century became accepted in Judaism at large in later generations as part of the Jewish cultural practice of Passover and is widely practiced today.

So how do we reconcile the passages from Matthew 26:17 and Mark 14:12 that seem to state clearly that the Last Supper occurred on Passover when it appears from other evidence that this event might have been something else? We must recognize that people are not always clear in their speech. Sometimes we say things that aren't explicitly true. It is common in the United States for the weeks surrounding Christmas to be referred to as "Christmas," even if it is not the actual day of the holiday. The statements made in these verses can be seen as similar to saying, "everyone came into town over Christmas, you know, when the gifts are opened," even though people arrived anywhere from the 20-24th of December and not specifically on Christmas day.

With all of this evidence I feel confident in stating that the Last Supper was in fact not a Passover Memorial, but rather was a traditional *seudah maphsehket* meal that signaled the beginning of a fast of the first-born that was part of a Galilean tradition. For anyone from

Galilee, these events were as much a part of the Passover observance as eating lamb or cleansing a house of leaven. But as I stated before, there is no way to be entirely certain.

The Passover Sacrifice

On the day of Passover, there were a series of events that were slated to occur as part of the temple service for the Passover lamb. One of the reasons that the High Priest was in such a hurry to be done with Jesus is because he was required to be part of these ceremonies. The sooner that he could finish the more time that he would have to prepare to lead the rituals. Fortunately, we have a decent timeline from the gospels to be able to pinpoint some of the events of this very busy day, but not all.

After the final dinner, Jesus and several of His followers went to the Mount of Olives which overlooks the temple grounds and faces the entrance to the temple. It was during the night that Jesus was arrested and His trials began. Throughout the night and into the next day, Jesus was subjected to five or possibly six different examinations by people in various positions of power.

In John 18:13 we read that Jesus was taken before Annas first. Now, remember, Annas was not the current High Priest. Annas, however, remained a power mover in Judea and continued to garner favor with Rome. He was still considered by many to still be High Priest, even if his son-in-law currently occupied the office. So when Jesus was arrested, according to John, He was not taken to the sitting High Priest first as the other gospels record. He was taken to the former High Priest and current High Priest in the eyes of many, Annas.

It was only after being taken to the home of Annas that Jesus was then taken before Caiaphas, an event that we read of in Matthew 26:57. It is while at the home of Caiaphas that three interesting things coincide in the timeline of Jesus's final day. First off, Peter, who had been following Jesus, was standing in the courtyard outside the house when he was approached by people who recognized him. It is during this trial that Peter denied Jesus three times before the rooster crowed. An event that was prophesied by Jesus the night before.

The second thing that occurred was the crowing of the rooster. Unfortunately for modern caricatures and cartoons, this was not a chicken. Mishnah *Bava Kama* 7.7 records that while the temple stood, chickens were not allowed in the city of Jerusalem at all. Chickens are dirty and they are capable of getting into even the most well-protected areas. Because of this, there was a fear that if chickens were in the city then they would find their way into the temple and make it filthy, so they were banned. But if this was not a rooster that crowed, then what is it that happened in this story that is recorded as a rooster? In this case, the description of a rooster is an idiom for the temple crier.

It was the job of the temple crier to call out at various times of the day to let those nearby know what was about to happen in the temple. This fact is recorded in many places including Mishnah *Tamid* 3.8 in which this individual is known as "Gevini the Announcer." The name gevini is a form of the word "gever," which means rooster in Hebrew:

> From Jericho, the people would hear the voice of Gevini the
> Temple crier, who would proclaim in the Temple each day:
> Arise, priests, to your service, and Levites to your platform,
> and Israelites to your non-priestly watch.
> —Mishnah Tamid 3.8

Rooster was a nickname for the temple crier, and it was this rooster that was the first sound heard from the temple each day. His call informed everyone who was part of the temple service that it was time to start heading to the temple to begin the preparations for the day's activities. This places the trial of Jesus in the very early morning at dawn, but just before sunrise. This was at a time of day when people would have been finishing their morning routines and getting ready to head to work.

The third significant event that occurred during this meeting is found in Matthew 26:65 and Mark 14:3. Caiaphas, in the process of questioning Jesus, takes offense at something that Jesus said, and in his appearance of piety, he ripped his robes. This might seem like it is simply a cultural expression of great sorrow. We read of this practice in other places in the Bible. Ripping your clothes is a sign of grief or anguish. But the High Priest was supposed to be above the culture. The robes of his office were not just clothing. They were a sign of holiness and service to God:

> The priest who is chief among his brothers, on whose head
> the anointing oil is poured and who has been consecrated
> to wear the garments, shall not let the hair of his head hang
> loose nor tear his clothes.
> —Leviticus 21:10

The High Priest's garments were a symbol of service to God, and the act of ripping those robes served as a sign of disrespect for the office. We already know that the High Priest was an illegitimate puppet of Rome, but in case there was any doubt, Caiaphas took this action that immediately disqualified him from the office.

The confluence of these three events should not be lost on us. Peter denies Jesus and removes himself from His presence. The High Priest denies his own office as the legitimate leader of the temple before the whole Sanhedrin. And the call to come and begin the day of worship is made at this same time. Suddenly, Jesus is abandoned and left in the hands of those who claim to represent the temple who no longer do. Many things occurred on this day, but as the sun rose, veils were being stripped away and hearts were being revealed. In the midst of this, Jesus is pictured as being left alone among pretenders bent on His destruction.

So while Jesus's final day began with the Last Supper and then a trip to the Mount of Olives for prayer; times of fellowship and worship. His final day, according to the Greek and Roman reckoning of a day, at sunrise, began with betrayal, abandonment, and overt hostility.

In the trial before Caiaphas and the Sanhedrin, a verdict was reached of guilty and the penalty was leveled at Jesus of death. But the religious leaders of the Jews did not have the power in Roman-occupied Judea to enact the death penalty. This power had been taken from them in 6CE when Rome finalized their control over Judea. The Jewish authorities needed to get Roman authorization to carry out the sentence.

Once more we see the Jewish leadership portrayed as impotent. Their posturing of legitimacy represented by the High Priest and council is revealed as just that, posturing. They had no true authority as it had all been given to or taken by Rome in the decades previous. Because of this, Jesus was taken before the Roman governor so that His murderers might gain the legitimacy and authority that they did not have themselves.

First thing in the morning, Jesus is paraded to the Roman governor, Pilate, and brought before him for judgment. It is at this point that we get our first connection of Jesus to the Passover lamb on this final day. You see, in the temple service, before the priest would sacrifice the Passover lamb, he would present it to the people who were assembled for the sacrifice of their own lambs and he would declare over the lamb, "I find no fault." But this High priest was a puppet. He was an impotent actor who had invalidated himself from making any sort of judgment, and so it fell to the one with true authority to examine the lamb and declare, "I find no fault in this man." (Luke 23:4)

During Pilate's initial questioning, it was revealed that Jesus was from Galilee. Pilate truly wanted no part in this matter and so Pilate shoved this matter off on someone else. He sent Jesus to be questioned by Herod Antipas, the Galilean tetrarch. You see, Herod Antipas was never officially a king although he is referred to as such in the New Testament. Rather, he was the ruler of a quarter (the literal meaning of tetrarch) of the Hasmonean kingdom, namely the districts of Galilee and Perea. The term king when applied to Herod Antipas was a hold-over from his father, Herod the Great, who was the first king of the Herodian dynasty and the last official vassal king of Rome in Judea. Once again Jesus was paraded before a puppet ruler who was simply an appointee of the Romans. When Jesus went before Herod he remained silent. He refused to acknowledge Herod's authority to have any say in His verdict, and so Herod quickly returned Jesus to Pilate:

> Pilate then called together the chief priests and the rulers and the people, and said to them, "You brought me this man as one who was misleading the people. And after examining him before you, behold, I did not find this man guilty of any of your charges against him. Neither did Herod, for he sent him back to us. Look, nothing deserving death has been done by him."
> —Luke 23:13-15

Neither Pilate nor Herod found fault in Jesus. Once again, those who had authority over the life of Jesus declared Him to be without fault as was the custom of the High Priest over the Passover lamb.

Despite the declaration of innocence over Jesus by multiple authorities, the crowd persisted in their insistence on death, and so a tradeoff was made. Barabbas, a legitimate murderer and rebel to the rule of Caesar, was let free. Jesus was paraded through the city and at the third hour, around 9 AM by modern reckoning, Jesus was crucified (Mark 15:25). At the same time in the temple, the morning sacrifice was being offered on the altar. For six hours Jesus hung on the cross in absolute agony.

Around 3 PM was the usual time for the evening sacrifice in the temple in the first century. On festival days, especially on Passover, thousands of sacrifices were expected. As an accommodation for this, the time of the evening sacrifice would be moved up an hour or more to allow for enough time for everyone to sacrifice, get home, and begin cooking the lamb before sunset. The evening sacrifice was not limited by a certain time of day. Remember that the command for this sacrifice was that it was to happen "between the evenings." All that was seen as necessary to fulfill the command of "between the evenings" was for the sun to begin to set. Imagine the surprise when the sun went dark at the moment that the sun began its descent in the sky. Those well versed in the scriptures, as the priests would have been, would have immediately thought of the prophecy of Amos:

> And on that day," declares the Lord GOD, "I will make the
> sun go down at noon and darken the earth in broad daylight.
> I will turn your feasts into mourning and all your songs
> into lamentation; I will bring sackcloth on every waist and
> baldness on every head; I will make it like the mourning for

an only son and the end of it like a bitter day.

—Amos 8:9-10

This prophecy speaks of the sun darkening at noon, and joyous celebration becoming a day of mourning like the mourning that accompanies the death of an only son.

Three hours later at the ninth hour, or 3 PM, the normal time of the evening sacrifice in the temple, Jesus finally died. In the temple, the Passover sacrifices were not begun until the evening sacrifice had been completed. The priests would sacrifice the national Passover lamb first before moving on to the individual sacrifices of the worshipers. The first Passover sacrifice in the year of Jesus' death, was none other than Jesus himself.

Throughout this day, from the trials and the declaration of innocence by the authorities to the timing of both crucifixion and death, His final day modeled the temple service of Passover. Jesus truly did fulfill the conditions of Passover. As I have already discussed, however, Passover did not stop on Passover day. The term Passover became an all-inclusive term for the entire eight days of celebration from Passover day through the end of Unleavened Bread. Just as Passover does not end on Passover day, so also Jesus's fulfillment of the conditions of Passover did not end at His death.

Which Sabbath?

The gospels state that the day following Jesus' death was a Sabbath, which led to the tradition that Jesus was crucified on a Friday. But as has been established, a Friday crucifixion does not allow for three nights in the grave, as well as several other logistical issues when it comes to determining a timeline for these events. This interpretation only allows for one Sabbath to occur during the week of Passover, but that is not the case in most years.

Each of the festivals that are described in Leviticus 23 has connected to them a day in which a person was not to engage in their normal labor. Unlike the Sabbath, this day was not necessarily meant for rest. Instead, it was intended to be a day of celebration and worship, and no one was to be prevented from participating in order to fulfill responsibilities towards others. During the second temple period, days of no work that were connected to the festivals became known colloquially as High Sabbaths. We find mention of the High Sabbath in John's account of the crucifixion:

> Since it was the day of Preparation, and so that the bodies would not remain on the cross on the Sabbath (for that Sabbath was a high day), the Jews asked Pilate that their legs might be broken and that they might be taken away.
> —John 19:31

There it is: "for that Sabbath was a High Day." The next day, which began at sundown, was a High Sabbath, not a normal weekly Sabbath. It was the first day of Unleavened Bread when the Passover Seder would be eaten by the people of Israel.

But how can we be sure of this? Perhaps the following day was both a normal weekly Sabbath as well as a High Sabbath. This does happen. A High Sabbath and weekly Sabbath do coincide every once in a while, so perhaps this is the solution! But the gospels describe two separate Sabbaths during this week. All we have to do is to follow the women and the spices as recorded in several of the gospels to see it, otherwise, we will miss it entirely.

In Matthew 27:27-61 we read that Joseph of Arimathea requested the body of Jesus so that he could bury Him before sundown. We find in v61 that Mary Magdalene and the other Mary sat across from the tomb and watched as Jesus's body was entombed. In this passage, we read nothing of the body being prepared other than it was wrapped in linen. The women apparently noticed something they thought had been overlooked and so they decided to take it upon themselves. The body had not been prepared with the traditional spices for burial. The spices that are referred to here were a series of herbs that were used to help mask the scent of a decaying body.

In Mark 16:1 we pick up the story of the spices as Mary Magdalene, Mary the mother of James (presumably the other Mary from Matthew), and Salome go out and purchase the necessary spices for the anointing:

> When the Sabbath was past, Mary Magdalene, Mary the mother of James, and Salome bought spices, so that they might go and anoint him.
> —Mark 16:1

Based on this account, it is possible to suggest that these three women went to purchase spices on Saturday after sundown, prepared them at home, and then went to the tomb early the next day to anoint Jesus. If this were the only verse that spoke to this subject then the reasoning would be sound in light of the tradition, but then there is this in Luke:

> Then they returned and prepared spices and ointments. On the Sabbath, they rested according to the commandment.
> —Luke 23:56

The women prepared the spices and then rested on the Sabbath. So did they get the spices before the Sabbath and prepare them, or did they wait until after the Sabbath to go purchase them and prepare them?

The only way that both of these verses can be true is if the tradition is wrong and two Sabbath days occurred during this week. The first Sabbath is the High Sabbath of the first day of Matza, then a normal weekday after, and then a weekly Sabbath. What is so very interesting is that these women did not need to purchase or prepare any spices at all. In John 19:39, we find that Nicodemus had already brought and prepared the body with the proper spices. This entire event of the women going to get spices was unnecessary, and yet it is recorded in multiple gospels, and it is from these inclusions that the timeline from death to resurrection can be established.

The sequence of events would look something like this. Jesus was crucified on the day that we currently call a Wednesday. His body was removed from the cross and entombed before sunset on this day. The women mentioned above saw this and thought that the body had not been properly prepared because there was not enough time to do so. What they did not know was that Nicodemus had taken care of this when they weren't watching. Because it was afternoon on Passover there were no vendors remaining open in the city or surrounding countryside to sell the necessary spices. So the women went to the place where they would memorialize Passover. Since the next day was a High Sabbath, they rested on that Thursday and were unable to secure any spices. The following day, on Friday, the women went out and purchased and prepared the spices for burial, but because of the guards on the tomb, or simply running out of time, they were unable to attend to the body on that day. When the weekly Sabbath came again at Sunset they rested once more according to the command.

Then, early on Sunday morning, before sunrise, the women went to the tomb to finish preparing the body only to find it missing.

A simple misunderstanding that the thing that they had spent so much time preparing to do had already been done, led to these women being the first to discover the empty tomb, and it is this that also gives us the keys that we need to unlock this timeline.

The Wave Offering

This timeline makes sense only if the ritual of waving the first-fruit offering, which is described in Leviticus, occurred on the day after the weekly Sabbath. As was mentioned in part one, there is some disagreement as to which Sabbath Leviticus 23 refers to when it describes the ritual of the first-fruit offering. This day is either the day after the High Sabbath or the day after the weekly Sabbath. If Jesus died on a Friday and rose on a Sunday, then this becomes a non-issue as that Sunday would have fit both interpretations. But if He died on a Wednesday, as the verses describing the actions of the women in relation to the burial spices, then the Sabbath referenced in Leviticus 23:11 can only be the weekly Sabbath.

When we approach the resurrection from the aspect of the first-fruits wave offering, we discover that Jesus continued to fulfill Passover in the Resurrection. In the temple service, early on the morning of the first-fruit offering, the High Priest would leave the city and go out into the fields surrounding Jerusalem. He would go to a preselected barley field and gather pre-selected stalks of ripe barely and bundle them into a sheaf for the offering. He would then return to the temple for the first-fruits wave offering ritual. In this ritual, the priest would stand before the altar, facing the Holy Place, and wave the sheaf of barley vertically. It was only after this ritual was complete that any of the new crops of barley could be eaten by anyone in Israel.

This wave offering served as a symbol of the first part of the harvest for the entire year being offered to God as a form of tribute of the best of the best. When we get to the gospels and read the accounts of Jesus's interactions with Mary Magdalene at the grave and the other disciples on the day of His resurrection, we gain a deeper understanding of the fulfillment of this ritual that simply served as a shadow of a greater reality.

The women arrived at the tomb early that Sunday morning. In some gospels, this is just before sunrise and in others, it is after the sun had risen. Regardless, when they got there the stone that sealed the tomb had already been rolled away. Two angels met the women and declared to them that Jesus had risen from the dead. At this news, the women ran back to the disciples and shared the news with them and several of the disciples then joined the women as they returned to the tomb to verify for themselves that He was missing. After the disciples verified the absent body of Jesus and returned to the place where they were staying, Mary Magdalene stuck around in the vicinity of the tomb crying. While she was there Jesus approached her and revealed Himself to her. When He did, He said something interesting that often gets overlooked:

> Jesus said to her, "Do not cling to me, for I have not yet ascended to the Father; but go to my brothers and say to them, 'I am ascending to my Father and your Father, to my God and your God.'"
> —John 20:17

The Greek word that is translated as cling here is the word *haptomai* (ἅπτομαι), which simply means touch. Do not touch me, Jesus said. Why would Jesus ask this of Mary? I submit that this request was made because Jesus had yet to fulfill the role of High Priest who was to avoid human contact on the day of first-fruits prior to the sheaf wave offering. If this is the case, then Jesus was fulfilling not only the role of the High Priest but He was also fulfilling the role of the wave offering as well. Paul speaks of Jesus as the first-fruits of the resurrection in 1 Corinthians 15:20. How can we know this? Later that day, when Jesus appears to His disciples, we find that he had no problem with being touched:

> And as they went to tell his disciples, behold, Jesus met them, saying, All hail. And they came and held him by the feet, and worshiped him.
> —Matthew 28:9

While at the tomb, Jesus prohibited Mary Magdalene from touching him, but later, when the disciples had returned to the place they were staying, he allowed them to touch his feet as they worshipped him. What changed in that time? He ascended to the Father. He ascended and then descended, describing a vertical line connecting Heaven and Earth. The same motion that was made with the sheaf in the hands of the High Priest. But is it possible that Jesus was not alone as the first-fruits of the resurrection? At the moment of His death, we read in Matthew 27:51-53 that a series of events occurred. The veil of the temple ripped from top to bottom, there was an earthquake of significant size that broke rocks, and many tombs were opened. It was only after the resurrection that it was discovered that some of the inhabitants of these tombs were resurrected alongside Jesus. These individuals went into the city of Jerusalem and were seen publicly by many (Matthew 27:52-53). I submit that these others who were also resurrected at this time may have served as part of a first-fruits wave offering of the resurrected dead that ascended before the Father. While there is no verse that states this outright, it does fit the pattern of the first-fruits wave offering.

It is because of this that the celebration of Easter is a completely redundant addition to the calendar of Biblical memorials (more on this in the next chapter). There is already a day in the Hebrew feast cycle that served as a shadow of the resurrection 1500 years before the events of this day. Around the world, many Torah Observant communities continue to observe this day. It is observed no longer as a practice of waving first-fruits of barley, but rather as a celebration of the resurrection of the one who is the first-fruits of our hope. This day is perhaps the least and most humble day of the festival cycle described in Leviticus 23 and yet has become the most honored day of remembrance. The promise of redemption and new creation has found its source. The first-fruits have been offered. Now we simply await the greater harvest.

Three Days

This timeline allows for Jesus to have been in the grave for three days and three nights, as he had stated he would be. His prophecy that was given as the sign of Jonah would then be fulfilled completely. But this timeframe of three days does not occur only in the story of Jonah. It takes a bit of inference, but "three days" was also part of the Exodus story.

As the Israelites journeyed from Egypt towards Mt. Sinai, they made three stops during the initial leg of their trip: Sukkot (Exodus 12:37), Etham (Exodus 13:20), and Pihahiroth, between Migdol and the sea (Exodus 14:2). It was at this final location that they were stopped by the Red Sea and could move no further. Ok, sure, they camped three times, but that does not necessarily mean that it was three days. That is beside the point. The point is the parallel between the two narratives, and these three stops serve as their own shadow of the Messiah. In the Exodus account, it was three stops between the Passover Sacrifice and the final defeat of the enemy. It was only when Israel reached the other side of this sea that the fullness of the new creation of the nation of Israel was realized.

The same thing is true in the narrative of the death and resurrection of Jesus. At the crucifixion, the Passover lamb of dedication was offered on behalf of all Israel. We as believers were set free from sin and death, but death still pursued. The Lamb had taken death into Himself, but death still reigned. During this time between, death still seemed to be powerful and have dominion over mankind. Then on the third day, rather than an impassable sea being parted, the earth was parted and Jesus walked out. He had become a new creation for the world to see. And not just to see, but to emulate. All who choose to follow this new Moses through the waters of death will find new creation on the other side.

Timeline of Fulfillment

With all of this data, we can finally construct a timeline for Jesus's final week. On Saturday the 10th, the day that the lamb was selected, Jesus entered Jerusalem. Some of the people waiting were there in expectation of Jesus's entry as a king. Also present were plenty of others waiting for the Passover lamb. Upon entry to Jerusalem, Jesus immediately went to the temple, but it was too late to accomplish anything, so He returned to the home of Lazarus in Bethany (Mark 11:11). The next day, Sunday the 11th, Jesus returned to the temple, and during the day He cleansed the house of God of leaven before once again returning to Bethany.

On the 12th, Jesus went into the temple, and during His time there His authority was questioned and defended. He spoke a minimum of three parables, He was approached by each of the major sects in attempts to trap Him up in word games which He deftly handled, and He took the opportunity to teach the gospel and the Kingdom of God. It was during this time that Jesus then spoke openly of the destruction of the Temple and gave signs of the end of the age. In this, the Lamb was inspected and examined fully by all parties concerned and no fault was found in Him. It was likely on this night that Judas approached the religious leaders of Israel and struck a deal with them to hand Jesus over to them in exchange for thirty pieces of silver.

On the 13th, as Jesus approached Jerusalem, rather than going to the temple He instead secured a place in which to "hold the Passover." The rest of the day was spent in preparation for the upcoming Passover, which He knew He would not get to eat. That evening as the sun set and Passover began, Jesus ate His final meal, truly a Last Supper as part of the Galilean tradition of the Fast of the Firstborn. It was at this meal that the practice that has become known as communion was begun and the practice of foot-washing was first commanded (John 13:14).

After dinner, Jesus and His disciples went out of the city for a time to the Mount of Olives. While on the Mount of Olives, Jesus spent time in prayer alone as the disciples continually fell asleep. During this time of intense prayer and pressure, Jesus sweat blood and pleaded for the cup that was about to be poured out to be taken away from Him. As the night neared morning, Jesus was approached by Judas leading the temple guard and He was arrested and taken into custody.

Over the next four to six hours, Jesus was subjected to either five or six trials. He was first taken to see Annas, the previous High Priest and one of the most powerful people in Judea. We aren't told of what occurred in this meeting, and only the gospel of John records it. After Annas, Jesus is taken to the home of Caiaphas where Matthew records that the elders had gathered to try Him. Here it seems as if this is a single event, but in the book of Luke, Jesus is taken to Caiaphas' house and held there until daybreak when the Sanhedrin convened to hold a proper trial. Is this one trial or two? Is the High Priest in Luke Annas or Caiaphas? In reality, it doesn't matter as it was while Jesus was at the High Priest's house that Peter denied Him, Caiaphas tore his robes, and the temple crier called out to assemble all of the priests and Levites who were to participate in the temple rituals for the day.

After daybreak, we can be sure that there was a trial before the Sanhedrin where Jesus was found guilty, but because of the impotence of this council, they could not carry out the judgment that they had determined. Due to this, the proper Roman authority had to be granted to carry out the death penalty, and so Jesus was taken before Pilate.

While before Pilate, Jesus was declared innocent of any charges that might deserve the penalty of death. During this trial, the priests mention that Jesus is from Galilee. Pilate sees this as a way to escape the responsibility of deciding Jesus's fate and shoves the whole matter into the lap of Herod. Herod, the Roman equivalent of governor in Galilee, was in town for Passover, and so Jesus was taken before Him.

When Jesus appeared before Herod He remained silent. It was apparent to Him that Herod wanted nothing more than a show and Jesus was not going to oblige. Herod quickly became bored with Jesus's noncompliance to his desires and sent Him back to Pilate.

During this second trial with Pilate, Jesus was declared innocent once again. At this point, it was pointed out that even Herod did not find fault with Jesus, so there were no grounds for execution. The conspirators persisted and had gathered a crowd to support their cause.

Due to the persistence of the Jewish leaders and the pressure of the crowd, Pilate was eventually persuaded to execute Jesus and to set Barabbas free.

What ensued at this point was a series of beatings, shaming, and punishments that would bring even the strongest person to the brink of death. After He was forced to carry the instrument of His execution through the streets to calls of mocking and slander.

By 9 AM on Passover morning, Jesus was nailed to the cross in the cruelest method of one of the cruelest forms of government-sanctioned execution in history. As He was being nailed to the cross, the morning sacrifice was being offered in the temple. For six hours Jesus hung on that instrument of torture after having undergone one of the most torturous beatings a human can experience.

After only three hours on the cross, at noon, the time when all work ceased in Judea and everyone began their final preparations for Passover, darkness descended on the area for three hours. During these three hours of darkness, no sacrifices were offered in the temple. Every part of the temple observance of Passover was put on hold until the darkness lifted when Jesus died. Upon His death, the veil in the temple tore from top to bottom, a significant earthquake was experienced, and many tombs in the vicinity of Jerusalem were opened. Because of the impending festival, none of these things were able to be addressed until Passover had passed.

Upon Jesus's death, His body was removed from the cross and given over to Joseph of Arimathea who, with the help of Nicodemus, prepared the body with the necessary spices and then wrapped the body in linen and placed it in the tomb. Nearby, Mary Magdalene and Mary the mother of James watched as Jesus's corpse was placed in the tomb, but they did not see that the preparation of the body with spices had already been accomplished. Because of this supposed oversight, the women were determined to accomplish this for Jesus. Since work had already ceased and all the shops were closed, there was nothing that they could do until Friday. That night they went and spent a Passover in grief and mourning with the disciples and those who knew and loved Jesus.

On the first day of Matza, while the rest of the city refrained from work and spent time with family and friends, either in mourning the death of Jesus, or celebrating Passover, the chief priests went to Pilate. It was no secret that Jesus had predicted that He would rise from the dead in three days and so they requested that a guard be placed at the tomb and that it be sealed. The last thing that they wanted was for Jesus's disciples to simply walk off with the body and claim a resurrection. Pilate agreed to this request and guards were posted at the grave.

On Friday the 16th, the women went out and purchased the necessary spices and prepared them while they also prepared for the upcoming weekly Sabbath. For some reason, they did not take the time on Friday to go and prepare the body. This was likely because the grave had been sealed and no one was allowed access to the grave until three days had passed. So Friday night and all Saturday the 17th, everyone once again observed a Sabbath, this time a weekly Sabbath rather than a High Sabbath.

At some point during this night, Jesus rose from the dead, folded His linen burial cloths, and escaped the tomb. Before sunrise on Sunday the 18th, the women came to the tomb and found it standing open and vacant. Immediately the women returned to the disciples and told them what they had found at the tomb and they all then went to the tomb to see. When the disciples had seen the tomb and then left, Mary Magdalene stayed behind weeping and was greeted by the resurrected Jesus. During the conversation, Jesus stated that he was not to be touched because he had not yet ascended to the Father.

When Mary left and returned to the others, they did not believe her until Jesus appeared to them. At this point, they all fell before Him and worshiped, while worshiping they touched Him. This day was auspicious in Jerusalem as it was on this day that many more people in the city of Jerusalem were surprised with the return of loved ones and saints. Other individuals who had been part of that first-fruits offering had been returned from the dead alongside Jesus.

Passover Fulfilled

This timeline is the only one that seems to fit the majority of the events that are recorded in the gospels. The issue of "three days and three nights in the earth" is resolved. No longer is it just the three partial days and two nights of the traditional timeline. Both verses discussing the women's interactions with the spices are accounted for. The Last Supper is placed within the first century Galilean context of the seudah maphsehket for the Fast of the Firstborn. And in all of this, from the selection and inspection of the lamb, to the sacrifice on the 14th and resurrection on firstfruits, every event of His final week serves as a fulfillment of the Passover rituals in ways that are much more profound than any physical memorial meal can accomplish. But as I opened with, there are issues with this timeline as there are with all of them. This view is also the only view that accounts for Mark 14:1-2.

> It was now two days before the Passover and the Feast of
> Unleavened Bread. And the chief priests and the scribes were
> seeking how to arrest him by stealth and kill him, for they
> said, "Not during the feast, lest there be an uproar from the
> people."
> —Mark 14:1-2

It makes no sense for Mark to include this insight into the plans of the priests and scribes and then not provide any reasoning for why they were unable and were forced to do it during the festival. The simpler answer is that the priests and scribes succeeded in their plans and had Jesus on the cross before the morning sacrifice on Passover. Thus they would be free to engage in their duties for the day and there would not be widespread riots due to an execution occurring on a High Sabbath.

With this view, Matthew 26:17, Mark 14:12, and Luke 22:7 are the only casualties that must be accounted for. As we have seen, the statements made in these books can be read as attempts to describe the entire festival and are not necessarily attempting to pinpoint a certain day. It is my opinion that this is how these verses were intended to be understood as Matthew 27:62, Mark 15:42, and Luke 23:54 refer to the crucifixion as occurring on the day of preparation. These three verses in each of the Synoptics are the only verses that seem to contradict this timeline, and even this is not the case.

An Alternate Timeline

But this is not the only timeline. The next most probable timeline of events is the current traditional understanding of the sequence of events with a Friday crucifixion and Sunday resurrection. There is a reason that this tradition has held so firmly for millenia, and that is because it does fit the recorded facts very well if understood plainly. As was stated before, any attempts at an accurate timeline will result in some verses being excused or described away. The only issues that need to be resolved in this understanding is Matthew 12:40 and the sign of Jonah. Rather than the words of Jesus being literal, this view sees this prophecy as symbolic. It is not the letter of the prophecy of three days and three nights that matters, but the spirit of the prophecy of three-days that matters. Alongside this, the various descriptions of what occurred with the spices can simply be chalked up to a disagreement between authors who witnessed different things, or who assumed that someone else took care of the spices. And the pattern of the week, such as the triumphal entry occurring on a day other than the 10th simply doesn't need to be associated with Passover at all.

Regardless of whether you agree with a Friday crucifixion or a Wednesday crucifixion or another day of the week should not matter. Whether Jesus was crucified on Passover, or on the first day of Matza is also a non-issue. Every New Testament author who speaks on these events makes sure to connect the crucifixion to Passover. What should truly matter to all believers, then, is that Jesus is our perfect Passover Lamb. He is without spot or blemish, and it is His blood that turns back the destroyer of our souls. His death frees us from the bondage of sin and death as we are then led through the waters of redemption. His power over life and death destroys the one who pursues, and in Him, we are a new creation. Through His blood we are invited into a new nation; one that was founded by God and whose King is God. His is a nation that is to be a light to all other nations. We who are of His nation should seek to call others out of darkness and into His marvelous light. Jesus, in His resurrection, has become the first-fruits of this new creation and the great symbol of our own hope for resurrection one day. He is the first of many to be resurrected from the dead His life demonstrates the faithfulness of God to bring about His promise of eternal life for all who swear allegiance to Him.

Passover is more than simply a story of freedom from slavery that occurred millennia ago. It is more than the story of salvation that is found in Jesus. Passover is our story. The story of all who would join themselves to Jesus. It is a story that belongs to each of us as individuals. It is a story of the entire community of God. It is our story, and as such, it is a story that we have the opportunity to engage in today.

PART 3

PASSOVER AND YOU

The year was 2011. My wife had just received some of the most devastating news of our lives. Her doctor was discharging her from his care and she was not expected to live much longer. This news was so devastating to me personally that my entire outlook on life was shattered. The web of faith that I had built up around the ability of doctors, medicine, and the good nature of God began to spider web into every aspect of my life. Things that I thought I knew and that I held to be true were challenged. Entire aspects of my identity were shattered. I was shaken to my core and floundering. My foundation was gone. My faith was gone.

After a week or so of floundering, I decided that I could not simply sit still. I had to move, to change. I had to rebuild what I believed, and I had to find help for my wife. So I devoted myself to the search. I could no longer rely on the faith of my father or the cultural institutions that I had previously accepted as my guides. I had to make my faith my own, regardless of where the path took me. My one prayer at this point in my life was, "God, if you are real, you are going to have to show me."

The year was 2014. I had finally arrived at a tentative conclusion of several years of intense study. My wife was in recovery from her sickness and I had come back to Christianity to a degree. Not the Christianity that I had been raised with, but a new (to me) form of Christianity that accepted all of the Bible as instructive for the Christian life. God had proven himself to me through this experience, and my own studies in science, philosophy, and religion had reshaped the way I looked at the world. I had won a hard earned certainty that God did in fact exist, and now I was determined to live my life according to His eternal principles.

As the spring of 2015 approached, my wife and I decided that our family would keep Passover, but we had no idea how. The Jewish synagogue in town was holding an event, but we felt extremely uncomfortable going into a synagogue that did not believe that Jesus was the Messiah for our first Passover experience. Instead, I did what I had always done when I had a question. I began to research how to engage in a Passover Memorial for myself. I found a Haggadah (a book with the order of Passover service) at a local used book store, and my small family of four kept our first Passover alone at home.

We had no idea what we were doing. Breaking the bread, reading the old English, telling stories of what Jewish Rabbis had to say about the specifics of Passover observance, attempting to sing a song that we had heard only a couple of times on YouTube. It was awkward and foreign. I stumbled through it and in the end it was beautiful. Despite the stumbling and awkward pauses while trying to figure out what to do next, this first Seder became a night to be treasured.

Since this first experience, the Passover Seder has become a highlight in our year. It is a time of family and community both somber and joyous. As we have gone through Passover year after year, I have realized that great truth of Passover. Passover is not just a distant event from the past that happened to "them," but rather, it is a central event in my own faith. As a Christian, I found that, just like Israel in the wilderness, I too was commanded to observe this feast (1 Cor. 5:8). But what does that look like? For many Christians, Passover is something that Jews do. We (Christians) celebrate Easter and they (Jews) celebrate Passover. I am not a Jew, so why would I celebrate this Jewish holiday?

As I explored this question, I found the beginning of an answer in the holidays listed in Leviticus. Often, when I heard of these festivals from others, they were steeped in terms such as "Jewish" holidays. An us-versus-them mentality that serves no one. But when I opened the Bible and read about these holidays, I discovered something profound. These are not simply Jewish or even Israeli festivals. Leviticus 23 states it clearly in its opening verses:

> The LORD spoke to Moses, saying, "Speak to the people of Israel and say to them, **These are the appointed feasts of the LORD** that you shall proclaim as holy convocations; **they are my appointed feasts**.
> —Leviticus 23:1-2

The festivals listed in Leviticus 23 are the festivals of the LORD. They are the festivals that are celebrated by the people of God. They are the eternal celebrations of an eternal God. They are not a cultural expression that is limited to a single people group. They are for all who join themselves to the God of Abraham, Isaac, and Jacob. These festivals are built into creation.

On the fourth day of creation in Genesis 1, God created the sun moon and stars and places them in the sky. The purpose of these items in the sky is stated clearly. "Let them be for signs and for seasons and for days and years." The word that is translated as "seasons" is the Hebrew word *moed* (מועד). This word literally means "an appointed or fixed time." This is the same word that is used in Leviticus 23. These are the *moedim*, the appointed times, of the LORD.

The festivals predate the giving of the Torah at Mt. Sinai, just as the Sabbath predates the Torah by being instituted at creation. Just as Paul makes the case that it is faith that brings salvation because Abraham believed before any law was given, so too, the festivals were built into creation before any law was created to codify these appointed times.

On the other hand, it is popular to say that the festivals are merely shadows and so we can easily dismiss them. This view is based on a verse from Colossians that I spoke on in part 2. But discarding a festival because it happens to be a shadow of the Messiah is to miss the most important part of these shadows:

> Therefore let no one pass judgment on you in questions of food and drink, or with regard to a festival or a new moon or a Sabbath. **These are a shadow of the things to come**, but the substance belongs to Christ.
> —Colossians 2:16-17

These are not shadows that have passed and are of no more use. These shadows are of things that are yet to come. Future tense to Paul. When Paul looked on the festivals and Sabbaths, He was not simply looking back at Jesus for the things that had occurred. He did not see their power and applicability ceasing with Jesus. Paul saw these festival days as looking forward to events yet in the future.

Let's go back to this shadow analogy from part 2. An object and its shadow cannot be separated. It is only when all light sources are removed that an object no longer has a shadow. Shadow, object, and light source are intrinsically connected. But what if an object is in the path of two or more sources of light? Well, an object that is placed in the path of multiple light sources can cast multiple shadows. The shadows of the Messiah can point to the past, but this same substance can also cast shadows into the future. In Passover and the other festivals, Paul saw signs that pointed forward as well as backward. He saw events that would occur again in one way or another.

Passover is not only located in the past. It is an event that is for all time. It is a shadow of future events. As we have already seen, Passover is an event that has occurred in the life of every believer. You were there. Your own salvation is a Passover shadow that points to the Messiah. As such, every Christian should make an attempt to memorialize this day and time. So why don't we? Why has the default of the church become an attempt to ignore Passover and focus only on the Resurrection? Well, the story of this change begins many centuries ago in the land of Judah.

A Brief History of the Early Church

The first century CE was a busy time for the church. When the century started, Jesus was only 2-3 years old. The only church at that time was the Jewish people in all of their divisions, arguments, and failings. Despite the terrible view that is popular of Jews being "snakes and vipers," at this time, there were many who were faithful God-fearers. Those who loved God in faith and who lived righteously. Zachariah and Elizabeth are two examples of this kind of person. Luke records that they were "both righteous before God," (Luke 1:6). There are many others who are recorded as having great faith or being righteous. Nicodemus, Lazarus, Martha and Mary, the disciples. The list goes on and on. In fact, most of the first believers in Jesus as Messiah were Jewish. Even the 3,000 that were added to the number on the day of Pentecost around 30 CE were all Jewish. Jews were all that the church had at its inception. Christianity began as a Jewish movement. It was not until Peter's vision in Acts 10 that the Jewish believers in Jesus even contemplated that gentiles might be a part of what God was doing in the world.

Even then, it was over a decade after the death of Jesus before the gospel was preached to gentiles in any real way. Paul and Barnabas were the first official missionary effort to the gentile world, and they left on their first missionary journey around 44-47 CE. Even so, pockets of believers began to pop up among gentiles before this journey. Luke wrote his gospel and the book of Acts at the request of Theopolis, likely a Greek patron who was interested in hearing more about Jesus. It is thought that John Mark, the most likely candidate for author of the gospel of Mark, founded the church in Rome before Paul ever stepped foot in Rome. In Acts 19 Paul encounters believers in Ephesus who had not even heard of the baptism of Jesus, and yet they are called disciples. The church spread like wildfire and it was all that the apostles could do to keep up with this growing body of believers. But it did not grow without opposition both internal and external.

All throughout the Epistles and other early church writings we read warnings against gnosticism, various forms of mysticism, and false teachers that began to spring up from within the church. The church father Iraneus points to Simon the Magus in Acts chapter 8 as the source of gnostic teachings. Justin Martyr condemned Simon in a letter to Emperor Titus, and then offered the Emperor a copy of his complete treatise refuting the teachings of Simon as heresies. Other heresies such as Marcionism, which discarded the Old Testament and all other books of the Bible except for the writings of Paul, began to be preached. Alongside these Gentile influences came Jewish heresies that taught that a person could not be saved without converting to Judaism. This view stated that a person had to go through the process of ritual proselyte conversion before they could be saved. And these are just a small sampling of the internal conflicts that faced the early church. Corruption of the gospel from inside the church became a real and present danger to the church very quickly.

On the other hand, the pressure on the early church was not solely internal. As the church spread, it began to face a lot of political pressure from Rome and from their Jewish and pagan neighbors. In 40 AD, before Christianity began to spread to the Gentile world in any real way, Emperor Caligula attempted to install a statue of himself in the Jerusalem temple. Caligula had begun to identify himself as Jupiter incarnate, and the statue was to feature both his name and the name of Jupiter. This move was opposed by many early Jews and Christians and the resulting riots created an animosity against all Jews from Rome. Because Christianity was seen as a Jewish sect, Christians also fell under this animosity.

Under the reign of Herod Agrippa I, the same Herod who served as tetrarch at the time of Jesus's crucifixion, James, the brother of John was martyred, and Peter was imprisoned. All throughout his reign there was a general animosity towards Christianity that was fostered. But when Herod Agrippa passed in 44CE, a period of 18 years passed in which the persecution of Jews ceased for the most part in Judea. But this was not quite the case in Rome.

Claudius succeeded Caligula as Emperor in 41 CE and under Claudius, the Empire was relatively accepting of both Jewish and Christian faiths. This does not mean that there was no friction. Claudius did expel Jews from Rome (Acts 18:2) after a series of violent incidents. The historian Suetonius stated that these incidents were "instigated by Christus." It seems as though there was a dispute that arose between Christians and Jews in Rome which resulted in some violence in the city. In response, Claudius simply expelled all Jews from Rome, because he saw it as an internal Jewish matter. From historical records it appears that Roman Empire of the time, while not liking either Jews or Christians, did not bear any specific animosity towards them, other than the animosity that was due to the frequent strife in Judea.

In 54 CE, the persecution of the church in the Roman Empire ramped up. Nero Claudius Caesar Augustus took the throne. Up to this point, Christians were unpopular in the Roman Empire. After all, they worshiped a man who had suffered a criminal's death. They claimed to eat His body and drink His blood. They refused to participate in rites that recognized the emperor as divine, and they were seen as lazy because they took an entire day off work every week. Because of this and more, Nero developed a distaste for Christianity as a whole. So when a massive fire broke out in Rome in 64CE, destroying two thirds of the city after burning for six days, Nero used Christians as a scapegoat to pin the fire on. Suddenly all Christians became public enemy number one. Christians were rounded up in Rome and were used as entertainment for Nero's dinner parties. Some were dressed in animal skins and wild dogs were unleashed on them until they died. Others were crucified throughout the city, and still others were burned alive to provide illumination for His parties and city streets. The charge that was leveled at Christians quickly evolved from a charge of starting the fire that had destroyed much of Rome to an assertion that Christians hated the human race (Tacitus, *Annals*).

While Nero's persecution of Christianity was limited to Rome, his actions set a precedent that was then followed throughout the rest of the empire. In many cities in the Roman Empire, Christians were persecuted in various ways which led to the first great influx of martyrs. Many second to fourth century Christian sources state that it was under Nero's persecution that both Peter and Paul met their end.[1] It is from the letter of First Clement that we first read of the martyrdom of both Peter and Paul but with no details. The expansion of this progrom against Christians is later attested in a letter between Emperor Trajan (98-117 CE) and Pliny the Younger. For the next several centuries, Christians faced persecutions of various sorts throughout the Roman Empire. Not as any Imperial decree, rather as localized policies throughout the Empire. Some areas were friendly, others were not to various degrees. It simply depended on the attitudes of those in power.

Despite this persecution and the internal strife that faced Christianity in the first century, the church grew. As part of this growth there was a lot of correspondence sent between various outposts of the gospel. Not only were all of the letters written by the apostles, which have become part of the New Testament canon, written at this time, there were other Christian writings that were distributed in the early church. The letter from Clement in Rome to the church in Corinth, which has become known as "First Clement," was written in 96 CE. This letter is the first extra biblical writing that we have has been reliably dated. Other early Christian works such as *The Didache, The Letter of Barnabas*, and *The Letter to Diognetus*, are some other early works that may predate "First Clement," but which do not have a reliable date attached to them.

The first century placed an overwhelming amount of pressure on the fledgling Christian church. For many looking in on the early Christians, they were nothing more than simply another sect of Jews. An odd sect to be sure, since they allowed gentiles to join without full conversion, but Jewish nonetheless. The practices of the church

1   Tertullian, *Scorpiace* 15; Lactantius, *The Manner in Which Persecutors Died* 2; Orisius 7.7.10; Eusebius, *Church History* 2.25; Dionysus of Corinth, *Letter to the Romans*.

remained rooted in the teachings of the Old Testament. Sabbath was still observed on Saturday. The Festivals were still observed. Synagogues were attended. The line between Jew and Christian was nearly nonexistent for the vast part of the first century.

It was in the late first and early second century CE when the church began to be established as a non-Jewish movement. Because of the influx of gentiles, a push came to separate Christians from Jews in various practices. This tendency for those outside of Judaism to lump gentile Christians into Judaism was simply too much, especially after the destruction of the temple in 70 CE. At this time an extra tax, known as the "fiscus Judaicus," was levied against the Jews of the Roman Empire. Anyone who was identified as a Jew was subject to this tax, and practices such as keeping the Sabbath were used to identify Jews. Anyone who paid the tax was exempt from the requirement to worship Roman gods, but the revenues gathered from this tax were used for the upkeep of the temple of Jupiter in Rome. Other onerous measures were implemented by the empire specifically against Jews as well. With the racial animosity that was ever present it is no wonder that those who saw themselves as different than Jews would seek to become different than Jews in practice. Out of this desire to be different rose many disagreements over how Christianity should rebrand itself. What lengths should this new movement go in order to become a completely separate religion? One of the first areas of contention to arise was the method by which Christians should observe Passover.

The Quartodecimen Controversy

In the early second century, the primary central location for church leadership was in the process of moving from Jerusalem to Rome. This move was occurring because of the increasing disassociation of Christianity from Judaism. During this shift, matters of observance became central. This is evident in a visit that occurred between Polycarp, the bishop of Ephesus, and Anicetus, the bishop of Rome in 155 CE. The episode was recorded by Eusebeus in his book, *Church History*. Now, this is a second-hand report as it was Irenaeus who originally recorded the event in a letter. This original letter, however, has been lost to history.

Eusebius recounts that during the visit of Polycarp to Rome he and Anicetus had a conference regarding "the question of the day of the Paschal Feast."[2] During this conference, Polycarp argued that Passover should be celebrated on the 14th day of the month, regardless of the day of the week on which it occurred. In his defense, Polycarp, who had been a disciple of John, took the position that this is what he had learned from the apostles. This is what John had taught him, and this is how Philip and other apostles whom he had met kept Passover. So, Polycarp saw no reason to change. Anicetus, on the other hand, took the stance that Passover should always be celebrated on Sunday, as this was the day that Jesus was resurrected from the dead. During the conference, neither side changed their stance, and they parted in peace. In fact, Anicetus allowed Polycarp to administer communion to the church in Rome before he left as a gesture of respect.

This interaction between two parties who disagreed on this matter became the cornerstone for Christian relations for the next several decades. Despite their disagreement on the proper day to observe Passover, those who chose to follow the command to observe it on the 14th and those who preferred to observe it on Sunday in recognition of the resurrection lived at peace with each other.

Thirty-five years later, things took a turn for the worse. The church held a series of Synods in Rome, Palestine, Pontus, Gaul, and

2   Eusebius, *Church History* bk4, 14:7.

Osrhoene. One of the questions addressed was the observance of Passover, and by unanimous decision, it was decided that the Passover should be kept on Sunday according to "Apostolic Tradition," and it is claimed that Peter began this tradition. Not everyone was happy with this decision. Bishop Polycrates of Ephesus, a disciple of Polycarp, voiced his protest in a letter to Victor, the bishop of Rome, regarding the decision made by the conference:

> We observe the exact day; neither adding, nor taking away.
> For in Asia also great lights have fallen asleep, which shall rise
> again on the day of the Lord's coming, when he shall come
> with glory from heaven, and shall seek out all the saints.
> Among these are Philip, one of the twelve apostles…and,
> moreover, John, who was both a witness and a teacher, who
> reclined upon the bosom of the Lord.
> —Eusebeius, *Church History* bk 5, 24:1-2

Polycrates continues in the letter, naming many more names of people who kept Passover, including several more actual apostles. In this letter he also states that he "put away the leaven" and provides his own qualifications as representative of the churches in Asia for sending this letter. In closing, Polycrates writes that they were not afraid of threats from Rome and that "it is better to obey God rather than man."

Victor was not pleased upon receiving this letter and responded harshly:

> Thereupon Victor, who presided over the church at Rome,
> immediately attempted to cut off from the common unity
> the parishes of all Asia, with the churches that agreed with

them, as heterodox; and he wrote letters and declared all the brethren there wholly excommunicate.

—Eusebeius, *Church History* bk 5, 24:9

Rome excommunicated all of the churches in Asia who continued to keep Passover on the 14th. These churches and anyone who kept Passover on the fourteenth became known as the "Quartodecimani," or "those of the fourteenth." Within a few decades, what was previously only a disagreement among brothers had become labeled as heresy by Rome.

This response became highly controversial in the church with several bishops, including Iraneaus, sending their own letter to Victor in protest. The protest was not over keeping Passover on Sunday. Rather, it was over excommunicating those churches who disagreed with the decision of the synods. In his letter, he makes it clear that these churches were simply keeping their own unbroken tradition that had been handed down by apostles.

Other bishops, including Narcissus and Theopolis from Palestine, as well as the bishops to Tyre and Ptolelmais, took it upon themselves to defend Victor's ruling by providing a defense of the observance of Passover on Sunday. In their letters, though, they all made an appeal for Victor to not go through with his decision to excommunicate all of Asia and, instead, to pursue peace, unity, and love.

No one really knows what happened at this point. The result was that the excommunication did not go through. Either Victor never followed through on the threat of excommunication, or he rescinded the edict quickly. After this point, little was said about this matter between various churches. Some believe that the practice of celebrating Passover on Sunday simply became the norm among all churches naturally and the quartodeciman practices died out. Others believe that this practice of celebrating Passover on the fourteenth continued in many churches for the next several centuries alongside the Sunday celebration of the event. In my opinion, the second view seems to be the more accurate because this issue is addressed once more in early church history.

Rome and the Early Church

Christian persecution was not the policy of the Roman Empire at all times. There were many decades where the Empire simply didn't care about Christianity in any real way. That is not to say that persecution did not exist in the following centuries, only that this persecution would occur at the local level of governors or prelates. The Empire simply didn't have a policy towards Christianity in any official capacity. That is until Emperor Diocletian.

In the late 200s, the Roman Empire was incredibly volatile and appeared to be near collapse. Then Diocletian came to power. In an attempt to stabilize the Empire, he split the Empire into four regions. Diocletian appointed Maximian as Emperor Augustus alongside himself, and they ruled over two of these regions. He then appointed Galerius and Constantius Chlorus as Emperor Caesar, a lesser title than Augustus, over the other two regions.

This arrangement proved to be fruitful, and stability was returned to the Roman Empire. For the majority of Diocletian's reign, Christianity was at relative peace with the empire. In fact, it is believed that Diocletian's wife and daughter were Christians. Everything seemed to be going well until 303 CE. No one knows what transpired to cause what happened next. We only know that in 303, Diocletian began a systematic persecution of Christians that had not been experienced up to that point. This time of persecution became so terrible that it has been named "The Great Persecution."

At first, Diocletian sought to capture Christian leaders without bloodshed and attempt to force them to apostatize. He knew the power of a martyr and he wanted to limit the number of Christian martyrs. His desire was to kill Christianity without killing Christians. This policy did not last long as the policy of the empire soon became one of total annihilation. Christian leaders were captured and given the option of offering a sacrifice to the emperor or any one of the Roman gods, or death. Extra favor was granted for anyone who turned over a Christian manuscript, which was then burned. Any buildings that were found to be places of Christian worship were burned to the ground, including the homes of many believers.

Diocletian persisted in this persecution until he abdicated the throne alongside his cohort Maximian in 305 CE. Despite the fact of Diocletian's abdication, this progrom of persecution continued under Galerius for another six years with even greater determination. Alongside this, the empire once again descended into chaos from the political maneuvering of those who sought to fill the power vacuum that was left by the retirement of two emperors at once. Despite the chaos that surrounded him, Galerius continued pressing the church. It was not until 311 as he lay sick on his deathbed that Galerius issued the Edict of Toleration, effectively ending the Roman Imperial policy of Christian persecution. He died five days later.

Upon the death of Galerius, Constantius Chlorus, also known as Constantine the Great, went into action defeating all usurpers to the throne of the western empire and uniting with Lucinius who was Emperor of the East. In 313 CE, Constantine and Lucinius together issued the Edict of Milan, going much further than the Edict of Toleration had gone. While the previous edict of Galerius had ended the Christian persecution, this new edict restored privileges and property to those who had been persecuted under the previous policy. Christianity was once again returned to a place of peace within the Roman Empire.

When the proclamation of tolerance was issued, two of the largest churches in 311 CE were in Rome and Alexandria. Due to the persecution of church leaders in the preceding decade, many churches were left without leaders, and the role of "metropolitan" was created to fill this void. A metropolitan was a church leader who oversaw multiple churches in large cities.

In 311 CE, the church leadership of Alexandria gathered together and began to reestablish a unified doctrine that was to be taught in the churches of the area. During this meeting, the question of the origins of the Son came up, and one man, Arius, insisted that if the Son was begotten by the Father, then the Son had a beginning and was not eternal. This stance drew the ire of Alexander, the metropolitan of the Alexandrian church. In 321 CE, ten years after the initial dispute, Arius was excommunicated from the church on grounds of this heresy.

Despite being kicked out of the church, Arius did not give up on arguing his viewpoint. As a poet he began to invent songs to be sung on street corners and marketplaces that presented his doctrine in a way that was accessible to commoners. During his crusade he was able to gather Eusebius, the bishop of Nicomedia, to his side. (This is not the same Eusebius that was a historian and bishop of Caesarea Maritima who is also referenced in this book.) With backing from Eusebius, Arius began to gain a following, and his teachings began to seep into the church. These teachings became so popular that Arius sought to found a church based on his own doctrines in competition to the existing church, and a civil war of sorts broke out.

Meanwhile, in 320 CE, Emperor Licinius, began ignoring the Edict of Milan and once again began persecuting the Christian church. Constantine saw this abandonment of Imperial policy as an opportunity to be rid of his rival co-emperor and a four year civil war was begun in the empire. Constantine, who was dealing with a schism in the Empire, recognized the threat that was posed by this schism in the church. Thus, he appealed to Hosius, the bishop of Cordova, to settle the dispute. This attempt failed, and so in 325 CE Constantine summoned church leadership from around the world to a council at Nicea that was intended to codify the doctrines of the church.

The Quartodeciman Ruling

When the council of Nicea gathered, they discussed many topics of doctrine as they attempted to forge their way forward. Questions on the nature of the Messiah and finer points of language used to describe these findings were the primary matters under discussion, but other issues were addressed as well. While Constantine did call the council together to settle these matters, he had no say in the rulings that the council made. But it must be recognized that the church had changed fundamentally from its inception. No longer was Christianity a religion that was based on the practices and commands of the Old Testament and a Jewish Messiah. Instead, this new version of the church was largely gentile and had become Roman-based and was meeting in council by decree of the Roman Emperor.

While the council settled many matters of doctrine in the twenty canons that were officially issued, the celebration of Passover was not addressed in this. Instead, the celebration of Passover was addressed in a letter that accompanied these rulings that was to be distributed among the churches throughout the world. This letter states the following:

> We further proclaim to you the good news of the agreement
> concerning the holy Passover, that this particular also has

through your prayers been rightly settled; so that all our
brethren in the East who formerly followed the custom of the
Jews are henceforth to celebrate the said most sacred feast of
Passover at the same time with the Romans and yourselves
and all those who have observed Passover from the beginning.
—Synodal Letter, Council of Nicea, 325CE

Although the council's rulings that were sent to the churches of
the world did not explicitly exhibit anti-Semitic tendencies, Constantine's accompanying letter indicated that the decision was motivated
by strong anti-Semitic sentiment:

At this meeting the question concerning the most holy day
of Passover was discussed, and it was resolved by the united
judgment of all present, that this feast ought to be kept by
all and in every place on one and the same day...And first
of all, it appeared an unworthy thing that in the celebration
of this most holy feast we should follow the practice of the
Jews, who have impiously defiled their hands with enormous
sin, and are, therefore, deservedly afflicted with blindness
of soul... Let us then have nothing in common with the
detestable Jewish crowd; for we have received from our
Saviour a different way... Beloved brethren, let us with one
consent adopt this course, and withdraw ourselves from all
participation in their baseness... Hence it is that on this point
as well as others they have no perception of the truth, so
that, being altogether ignorant of the true adjustment of this
question, they sometimes celebrate Passover twice in the same
year. Why then should we follow those who are confessedly
in grievous error?...Since, therefore, it was needful that this

matter should be rectified, so that we might have nothing in common with that nation of parricides who slew their Lord... but also that it is most fitting that all should unite in desiring that which sound reason appears to demand, and in avoiding all participation in the perjured conduct of the Jews.

—Eusebius, *The Life of Constantine*, 3.18-19

Constantine's letter makes it very clear that the reason for choosing to celebrate Passover on a Sunday as opposed to the fourteenth was so that the church would not model Jews in any form. The final resolution of the quartodeciman controversy was based on a desire to maintain unity in the church. But rather than unifying behind scriptural precedent and Biblical commands, the church decided to unify behind tradition and racism. According to Constantine's letter, the popular opinion was to not appear Jewish in any way, and so the celebration of Passover was codified into a Sunday observance.

While it is easy to criticize the church for making this decision based on these reasons, we must recognize the situation of the time. The church was attempting to define itself, not based on where it came from, but based on its own merit. In the attempt to accomplish this, it was settled that the Sunday on which the church's celebration would occur would be the Sunday after the 14th, unless that Sunday was the 14th. In that case, the celebration would occur on the following Sunday. The church did not want to be seen as celebrating the "Jewish" Passover even by coincidence. In reality, what the church instituted without realizing it was a church-wide celebration of first-fruits while still calling it Pascha (Passover in Greek). The terrible racial motivations that the bishops in the council held led to the church fully instituting a church-wide celebration of first-fruits!

Since then, Resurrection Sunday has become the default Christian celebration of the events of Jesus' final week. In English, this celebration is now called Easter. Easter itself is not bad or evil at its root. It was an attempt to celebrate the resurrection of Jesus in a way that was different from Jews, and it is, even today, first-fruits by another name. It is still as sweet. In fact, in many languages, including Greek, this Sunday celebration is still called Passover. In Bulgarian it is Paskha. In Dutch it is Pasen. Italians call it Pasqua. In Finnish this Sunday is known as Pääsiäinen. In Indonesian it is Paskah, and Portuguese calls it Páscoa. Likewise, the English name for this holiday of "Easter" has nothing to do with Ishtar as some have asserted. Rather the name Easter originated from the Germanic Oester, the month that corresponds to the English month of April. This is the month in which the celebration of both Passover and Easter usually occurs. The holiday simply became named after the month in which it occurred in Germany, and that convenation has carried on into English today.

It was the ruling of the council of Nicea that served as the final division between the Christian church and Judaism. But the divide between these two expressions of the faith of Abraham had been forming for centuries at this point. Judaism during this time was facing its own problems of persecution from the Empire, and when Christiantiy and the Empire became one and the same in the eyes of the world, the potential draw towards Christianity ceased for those who were Jewish.

A Brief History of the Fall and Exile of Judea

As Christianity was fighting to be born into the world, the world became increasingly hostile toward this faith. The idea that a man who was seen as a crucified criminal was the path of life and salvation was preposterous. At the same time, Judaism was fighting against its own extinction in the face of a world that despised these odd and contrary people. The animosity that many Jews felt towards the Romans in the days of Jesus only grew in the decades that followed. Rome continued to attempt to impose idol worship on the Jews. The situation with the statue of Caligula Jupiter that was to be placed in the temple in 40 CE is just one isolated example of this. Alternatively, the Jews continued to push back against Rome in an increasingly violent manner.

In 66 CE, during the reign of Nero, a full scale war broke out between the Jewish people and the Roman Empire. This war started when the Roman governor, Gessius Florus, plundered the Jerusalem temple in the name of the Roman Empire. The following day he then raided Jerusalem and arrested many prominent Jewish leaders. This action prompted a reaction by Jewish rebels that resulted in Rome being driven from the city. Immediately, Judah experienced a series of victories against Syrian legions that attempted to support the routed garrisons of Judea. By the end of 66, Judea controlled the majority of Judea, Samaria, and Galilee.

In response to this, Nero dispatched general Vaspasian in 67 to defeat the Jewish rebellion, and in that year, through patience and cautious planning, Rome was able to secure Galilee and Samaria. The defeated forces from Galilee flocked to Jedea and fortified Jerusalem.

This was a problem. Jerusalem was largely controlled by Sadducees who believed only in the Torah, and only extreme literal interpretations of the Torah at that. The northern forces, on the other hand, were composed primarily of Zealots who believed very similarly to Pharisees in matters of religious practice, but who disagreed to the point of violence on how to respond to the Roman occupiers. The differences between Sadducee, Zealot, and Pharisee viewpoints led to a miniature civil war in the city of Jerusalem that continued through the fall of the city.

The fall of Jerusalem began in early 70 CE when Vaspasian besieged the city. Because of the time of year, many pilgrims intent on celebrating Passover were trapped in the city. Tacitus, a historian, places the number of people in the city during the siege at 600,000. Josephus places this number at over 1 million. During the siege, everyone, man, woman, and child was armed for conflict that was seen as impending. Vaspasian quickly overcame the first two walls in the city, forcing all of the defenders into the smallest part of the city behind the third wall. The larger number of people in Jerusalem from all walks of life led to infighting among the city's defenders. At one point, in an attempt to get the garrisoned soldiers to attack the Roman forces, the Zealots burned the city's food supplies. Despite this, the soldiers in the city did not venture out in any great numbers, and the city refused to surrender to Rome. The only result of this action was that starvation in the city began before the final wall fell.

During the siege, Rabbi Yochanan ben Zakkai was secreted out of the city in a coffin by his disciples. Legend says that Rabbit Zakkai argued for peace while in Jerusalem during the siege. It was the anger of the populace that caused him to leave the city. Upon leaving the city, Zakkai is said to have met with Vaspasian. Zakkai and Vaspasian had been in contact during the siege and Vaspasian knew that Zakkai had been attempting to get the city to surrender. During this meeting, he prophesied that Vaspasian would soon become emperor. In response because of what Zakkai had attempted and the prophecy that he had given, Vaspasian asked what Zakkai wanted in return. Zakkai asked for the school that he later formed in Yavne.

When Vaspasian was informed of the death of Nero and that he had been selected as the new Emperor. Vaspasian returned to Rome and left his son Titus to continue in his place. It took nearly eight months, but in the end, Rome breached the walls of Jerusalem.

Leading up to the siege of Jerusalem, alongside the retreating northern forces and Passover celebrants, Idumean forces had come to the support of Judea and had become garrisoned within the city. When the walls finally fell, the Idumeans turned on their Jewish hosts in an attempt to garner favor with Rome. When Jerusalem fell, the people who remained in the city were slaughtered wholesale. The temple was plundered and then destroyed, and the entire city was burned.

It was the escape of Zakkai from the city that is credited as saving Rabbinic Judaism. When Zakkai had finally established his school in Yavne, he began the process of collecting and codifying the various written legal decisions up to that point, into what has become known as the Mishnah. Zakkai's escape from Jerusalem served as a pivotal event that paved the way for Judaism to continue millenia into the future despite the impending exile.

Several decades later in 115 CE, a second Jewish Roman war erupted. This time the war was not limited to Judea and the surrounding areas. In the eastern reaches of the Roman empire, Emperor Trajan was forced into war by an invasion of the Parthian Empire into Armenia. When the Roman legions were occupied in the east, Jews in Libya began to revolt against the Roman garrisons of the region. Not long after, Jews in Egypt, Crete, and Judea joined the revolt and before the end of the year, Jewish populations in Turkey, and what is known today as Iraq, rose up as well.

Throughout the Roman Empire, armies were dispatched to put down the various rebellions that had seized on this opportunity of perceived weakness, but it didn't last long. Within only two years, all of the revolts had been defeated and Rome had reestablished control. By then the damage had been done.

In Libya the damage was so extensive as to leave the country severely depopulated. It was so bad that historians record that the land would have reverted back to wilderness if Emperor Hadrian had not sent colonists in later years to reestablish a population. In Cyprus, historians record that over 240,000 Greek citizens were killed by the Jewish rebels. While the rebellion was put down, the result of the vicious slaughter of the Roman and Greek population was that Jews were expelled from Cyprus on the punishment of death. Alexandria in Egypt was burned and several Roman tombs were desecrated by Jewish forces. In response the people of Alexandria rose up and massacred its Jewish population, including those who had not participated in the rebellion. In Judea, the revolt was put down by Roman General Lucius Quietus after a few short battles in which the Romans overran rebel forces.

This violent and widespread rebellion throughout the Roman Empire resulted in widespread oppression of Jews. Despite this, Jews were allowed to remain in Judea and were permitted a measure of self autonomy and rule. But the Jewish population was growing antsy. They felt as if this had all happened before. When the first temple was destroyed it had been only 70 years before Babylon fell to an empire that was friendly towards them and they expected a similar thing to occur. Many Jews saw the Parthian invasion as the moment of this new empire rising up to supplant Rome. The various rebellions around the empire rose up in expectation of reestablishing a Jewish state and rebuilding a third temple and failed.

As the seventy-year mark since the destruction of the temple approached, Rome seemed as strong as ever. In 129 CE, Emperor Hadrian visited Judea. While he was there he promised to rebuild the temple in Jerusalem and established the Roman colony of Aelia Capitolina on the ruins of Jerusalem. It was later discovered that the temple that was being built on the site of the second temple was not intended to be a Jewish temple, rather it was to be a temple to Jupiter, causing a sense of betrayal among the Jews. Later Hadrian banned the practice of circumcision and began a progrom of Hellenization among Jewish populations.

Many devout Jews saw in these actions, parallels with the previous treatment at the hands of Antiochus Epiphenes and the Seleucid Empire. With the timing being right and the increasing oppression at the hands of the government, it was time to rise up and overthrow the oppressors in the manner of the Maccabees of old.

It began with small bands of rebels who had hidden themselves in caves in order to avoid the oversight of Rome. In 132 a revolt started which was led by Simon Bar Kozba. This rebellion found great initial success and was able to cut Jerusalem off from Roman support and then took the city. Bar Kozba set up a government in Jerusalem and declared an independent state from Rome. Because of this success and popularity, Bar Kozba was renamed Bar Kokhbah (son of a star) and was declared to be the Messiah. Jewish forces quickly drove Rome out of Judea and victory seemed to be at hand.

Emperor Hadrian had other plans. During the Kitos war of 115 to 117 Hadrian had been governor in Syria and had experienced the vicious uprisings of the Jews throughout the Empire. In fact, Hadrian became Emperor when Trajan died on his way back to Rome from his victory against the Parthians at the time. Hadrian's rise to power had occurred just after a widespread Jewish revolt, and so when this new Jewish revolt broke out, Hadrian dispatched six legions with auxiliary and support units from six other legions to deal with this threat.

The ensuing war was brutal with heavy losses inflicted on both sides. Two Roman legions were disbanded completely as a direct result, and heavy conscription occurred throughout the Roman empire to replace losses. Regardless, the Jewish toll was much higher. Historian Cassius Dio records that over 580,000 Jews died in the conflict with even greater losses due to famine and disease. 50 forts and 985 villages throughout Judea were also destroyed. After the war, vast swaths of the Jewish populace was sold into slavery. The destruction was so complete several modern scholars have likened the destruction of Judea to a genocide of the Jewish people.

This seems to have been the intent of Hadrian. After the victory, the names of Judea and Israel were changed throughout the empire, to Syria Palaestina. Jews were forbidden from the city of Jerusalem. Torah laws and the Jewish calendar were forbidden, and many Jewish scholars were executed. The temple to Jupiter was finished on the temple mount and sacred Jewish scrolls were burned ceremonially in the new pagan temple. Hadrian desired to completely root out all vestiges of Jewish nationalism and faith and did his best to turn everyone against the Jewish way of life.

It was during this rebellion that the divide between Judaism and Christianity grew the widest. The Roman Empire turned against many Christians because they continued to live in the Jewish way, observing Sabbaths and festivals and eating clean foods. Many Jews, on the other hand, turned against Christians as well, killing thousands, because they refused to support Bar Kokhba or declare him to be the messiah. This pressure from both sides pushed the Christian church to increase their abandonment of any sort of practice that looked Jewish as was already discussed.

In 135 CE, the exile of the Jews began. This people group in exile became known as the Diaspora as Jews moved from place to place while attempting to maintain their distinctiveness as a uniquely identifiable people.

Jewish Foundations for the Diaspora

The exile of Judah into the uttermost parts of the world created a unique set of challenges for the people of Israel. The Jewish people throughout the world were in danger of losing their faith and assimilating into their host nations. Recognition of the prospect of losing their identity caused many Jewish scholars and sages to work even harder to codify the religion in written form, and around 200 CE the Jerusalem Talmud was finished. Several centuries later, an updated and separate version of the Talmud was completed that is known as the Babylonian Talmud. These works served as the backbone of Jewish practice in later centuries as Jewish people groups were forced to move from place to place.

Alongside a wide recognition of the loss of identity came a recognition of a loss of time. No longer was there a governing body to declare dates and times. An issue which was vitally important for the continued celebration of the festivals. The calendar of earlier millenia was in danger of being lost to the widespread practice of the Julian and later the Gregorian calendars. The Jewish world was facing a similar challenge as the Christian. What could they do to ensure unity in time and practice, especially when it came to the holidays while scattered in the diaspora?

From the time of the destruction of the temple in 70 CE, various Jewish leaders had begun to use math to calculate the beginnings of months and years. Before this point, the calendar had been established through observation of the phases of the moon and agriculture. But now, outside of the land and with the prospect of exile looming, other avenues were being explored. No one is sure when it started, but by the final redaction of the Babylonian Talmud in 400 CE, a reliable mathematical model was in wide use—a calendar that is still in use today.

It was not until around the year 1000 CE that the calendar's creation was attributed to Hillel II, a Rabbi from the late fourth century. Other rabbis such as Nachmanades and Maimonodes, both late 12th century Rabbis, upheld this tradition claiming that the calendar was in wide use by 360 CE. Regardless of the validity of this tradition, the Hebrew calendar is today called the Hillel II calendar, or more commonly among those outside of Judaism, the Jewish calendar.

The codification of the Talmud and the creation of a mathematical calendar enabled Judaism to endure throughout the centuries of the Diaspora and have continued to provide a foundation for the religion until the present day.

Passover in the Diaspora

One of the challenges that was faced by Judaism in the Diaspora was the question of how to keep Passover without a temple or access to Jerusalem. Since the temple was gone, normal sacrifices could no longer be offered. Even those who saw Passover as an allowance for domestic sacrifice ceased because of lack of access to Jerusalem. The pilgrimage was not an option. How was this holiday to be kept?

The Talmud recognized this issue, and so it contains rulings on many of the finer points of Passover observance in tractate *Pesachim*. When is the final leaven supposed to be searched for on Passover? In the morning or in the evening? Read the Talmud and you will find long conversations on the merit of both ideas. How much light you need to conduct the search, and just how thorough the search should be are also addressed at length with various Rabbinic opinions offered. What day should the festival be held on as there is no way to be sure that you are on the right day? The answer: keep the festival two days to ensure that you celebrate on the right day.

The listings of these arguments are quite extensive and cover a hundred different topics. Out of these arguments arose the traditions that surround Passover observance in Judaism today. Many Jews recognized that the destruction of the temple occurred as a matter of Judgment on Israel for not keeping the Torah as God expected. Then came the exile from Jerusalem and the diaspora. These events were seen as the judgments of Leviticus 26 and Deuteronomy 28 coming to pass, and so the way out of this situation was to return to God in every way. This meant keeping the Torah as faithfully as possible and when possible, doing even better than the expectation of the Torah.

So when it came to Passover the rules became quite extensive. Bread dough could only sit around for eighteen minutes maximum before being put in the oven to bake, lest it have time to begin to leaven. Flour for Passover matza had to be put in special containers which were thoroughly inspected beforehand so that no leavening might occur in storage. The Passover Seder was required by custom to contain certain elements or it was not complete and thus thought to incur guilt. In some sects of Judaism, lamb should not be eaten because the Passover lamb was something that was done in the temple, and without temple or sacrifice, eating lamb for this occasion would be to treat the holy as profane. Because of these new traditions that were being built around Passover without a temple, a whole ceremony was created that accompanied the Passover meal. This ceremony is called a Seder.

The Origin of the Seder

The first mention of a Seder in Jewish writings is in the Mishnah Pesachim chapter 10. The word Seder simply means "order." This particular chapter is thought by many scholars to have originated either just before or just after the destruction of the temple. What is so very interesting in the Seder as it is described in Jewish literature and practiced today is their form. The practice of the Seder and the literary forms of the accompanying Haggadah have been found to resemble Greco Roman dietary habits and table manners from the early centuries.

This assertion was first made by Siegfried Stein in 1957 in the Journal of Jewish Studies[3] and has since been expanded on by various scholars who have written on the origin of the Seder. There is disagreement between these scholars as to the reasons for the creation of the Seder. One such scholar[4] asserts that the Seder was created as a replacement for the Passover Sacrifice and meal once they could no longer be accomplished. Yisrael Yuval on the other hand asserts that the Seder was created in answer to the rising Christian practice of celebrating the resurrection of Jesus with a communal meal.[5] His arguments stems from the existence of Greco Roman banquet elements that he believes were first introduced by Gentile Christians, and so when Jews decided to create their own they borrowed some of the Gentile Christian elements.

Regardless of the reason why the Seder was first developed, the correlations to an ancient Roman symposium are undeniable. The Seder as described in the Mishnah Pesachim chapter 10 states that the Shamash (servant) is the hero of the feast. The shamash is to bring the food to the table and Seder was not to begin until the wine had been brought. In Roman writings we find the same thing as servants were

3 Siegfried Stein, *The Journal of Jewish Studies* 8 (1957), 13-15.
4 Baruch Bokser, *The Origins of the Seder: The Passover Rite and Early Rabbinic Judaism* (London: University of California Press, 1984), 50-67.
5 Yisrael Yuval, *Two Nations in Your Womb: Perceptions of Jews and Christians in Late Antiquity and the Middle Ages*; (Los Angeles: University of California Press, 2006), 77-107.

to bring the food for a banquet and the banquet could not begin until the wine had been served.

Another item that is described in the Mishnah is that everyone who eats of the Seder was to do so reclining around the table. Reclining was to be done on the left side "as free and wealthy people eat." This custom of reclining while eating is a Greek practice during a banquet that can be traced back to the time of Homer in the eighth century BCE.

The Mishnah (*Pesachim* 10.1) states that a person must drink at least four cups of wine at the Seder. If one refrains they have not completed the Seder. Antiphanes in the fourth century BCE relates that when one is feasting they should honor the gods by drinking a minimum of three cups of wine.

The Mishnah (*Pesachim* 10:3) states that the shamash is to bring hazeret, which is lettuce or parsley, which is to be dipped in salt water or other liquids until the meal is served. This was a common practice in the ancient world and it is mentioned several times in Athenaeus' "Learned Banquet," which is a description of Roman food and drink of the second century CE.

The servant is also to serve Haroset with the meal as part of the banquet. This is an apple and nut mixture that is served as part of the Seder. A first-century BCE physician, Hericleides of Tarentum, describes very similar dishes and recommends that they be eaten as an appetizer, not a desert.[6]

The central and final part of any modern seder is the afikoman. This is a piece of matzah that is hidden in the course of the Seder. At the conclusion of the meal and its surrounding elements, the children of the Seder are set loose to go and find the afikoman, and the child

---

6   Stein, 16.

who finds it is usually rewarded with a prize. In the Roman banquet, at the climax of the festivities, the attendees would leave the place of their banquet and force their way into a neighboring home. They would then force the neighboring family, through food, drink, and merrymaking, to join them in their revel. This event was called the *epikomon*. What is curious is that in the Mishnah (*Pesachim* 10:8) it states that one may not add an afikomen after the paschal lamb, and yet, the hiding and search for the afikomen is widely practiced today.

What is even more poignant is that during the Seder four simple questions are asked as part of the ceremony. Plutarch, a Greek philosopher and historian of the first century, states that when one holds a banquet they are to ask questions of the guests, but the questions are to be "easy, the problems known, the interrogations plain and familiar, not intricate and dark, so that they may neither vex the unlearned nor frighten them."

The correlations between the Roman banquet, or symposium as it was known, and the Jewish Seder do not stop here. There are many other minor ways in which these events mirror each other, but these correlations grow increasingly disparate.

Just as the Christian celebration of Passover became increasingly influenced by Greek and Roman influences, so too, the Jewish celebration of Passover became influenced by Roman customs. But as was discussed in part 1, this was the case from the very beginning. The original Passover sacrifice was one which was known by those who participated. The Israelites would have felt some measure of familiarity as they offered the sacrifice at the threshold of their homes. God used elements that the people knew from the surrounding culture as He drew these people towards Himself. In the early church the same thing happened. Ceremonies and celebrations were created in both the Christian and Jewish faiths that incorporated familiar elements from the surrounding culture. A third century gentile would have felt comfortable at both a Jewish Seder held on the fourteenth of the Hebrew month, or at a Christian Pascha celebration which was held that following Sunday, because even if the content was different, the forms were familiar.

As we consider this divergence in memorial practices we find that neither celebration is truly consistent with the Biblical command and neither is a celebration that is completely untainted by outside influence. This inconsistency with what is written in the Bible is not a matter of disobedience as has been claimed by many in the modern world. Rather it was based on necessity of the times and the recognition that Passover, as described in the Bible, could no longer be accomplished. With no temple and not sacrifice the memorial prescriptions were impossible. This recognition alone should help to bridge the gap between the Jewish and Christian practices.

Not the Passover of Old

There is no way to keep the vast majority of the Biblical commands surrounding Passover in the modern world. The circumstances of the world prevent a true expression of Passover as it is written. We cannot sacrifice a lamb. There is no temple in which to offer the sacrifice. Even if one believes that the domestic sacrifice of lambs is the proper way, a person would need to be in Jerusalem in order to offer this sacrifice. A pilgrimage to Jerusalem is no longer necessary. Just as blood on the doorpost and eating in preparedness was not necessary after the first Passover, these other commands have become impossible in the present age.

This raises the question: is Jerusalem still the place where God's name dwells? Psalm 132:13-14 seems to indicate that Jerusalem will be the dwelling place of God forever. Yet in Lamentations 2, God rejects the temple, priesthood, and everything to do with them as they are taken into captivity, and in Ezekiel 10 the glory of God leaves the temple. In Zechariah 2:12-13, God declares that He will once again choose Jerusalem as His holy city. How can this be unless God rejected it during the exile? This leaves us with a conundrum. How can Jerusalem be the place that God has chosen as His dwelling forever, and yet He left it, rejected it, and will choose it again one day in the future?

To understand this we need to recognize that when a thing is said to last forever in the Bible, this does not indicate a continuity from eternity past into eternity future. Only the things that are eternal fall under this description. Something that is forever is a thing that God will return to over and over through this eternity, but which may not be continuous. Consider the throne of David as an example. In 2 Samuel 7:12-13 God states that He will establish the throne of David through His offspring and that this kingdom will last forever. But if this is the case, how do we understand the times when Israel was in Exile and there was no offspring of David on the throne? Unless, we understand that in the course of "forever" there may be times when the continuity is broken. There was a king on the physical throne of Israel in times past. There will be a king on the physical throne of Israel in times future, but at this moment, there is no king on the throne of a physical Israel. This does not make the promise any less of forever. We simply have to recognize that forever and eternal are not one and the same.

So where does that leave us today? Where is the place where God dwells? He dwells with His people. Ephesians 2:19-22 states that the church is being built up as a dwelling place for God, with Jesus as the cornerstone and the apostles as the foundation. Does this mean that we should sacrifice the lamb wherever we are? Yes and no. We are not to offer an animal sacrifice. Rather, the lamb is represented in Jesus, who has been sacrificed for our redemptions. So we can partake of that sacrifice wherever we are. His sacrifice frees us from the slavery of sin and death. As the author of Hebrews states, He was sacrificed once and need not be sacrificed again. All we need to do is accept His blood as the means by which we are counted as part of the Kingdom of God. Should we then go out and kill a physical lamb in our backyards since God dwells with us? No. The dwelling of God in the midst of the church is a spiritual dwelling and so the sacrifice that we offer on Passover is to be a spiritual sacrifice.

The fact remains that even if we were to attempt, we simply cannot sacrifice a lamb, and so all of the commands regarding the lamb are no longer achievable. The command to burn before morning or not break a bone have lost their physical counterpart. Added to this, the place where God's name dwells is not currently Jerusalem. It is in our local communities. We should still travel for the event, but rather than trekking miles to reach a city, we can go to the place that is being built as the dwelling place of God as Ephesians 2 describes it.

Because the lamb cannot be sacrificed in the prescribed manner, then it follows that the memorial meal as described cannot be accomplished as described. There is no need for ritual purity before partaking in the meal. Likewise, there is no need for a physical circumcision before eating. The circumcision that is necessary is a spiritual circumcision that is described by the idiom of a circumcision of the heart. We can still eat bitter herbs and matza as part of our memorial, but the event is not a Passover as described. It truly is a shadow of the reality that the Bible describes.

In fact, one of the main items on the list of commands that we might be able to properly accomplish in the modern world is to celebrate on the correct day, but alas, even deciding this comes with complications.

In the New Testament, Jesus kept Passover according to the command. We know this because He was without sin. Failing to observe Passover as it was commanded was an action that, in Numbers 9, would result in a person being cut off from Israel. So we know that Jesus kept Passover on the correct day. Now, we know that in the first century the beginning of a month was set when the first sliver of the moon was seen in the Western sky just after sunset. The process of declaring the beginning of the month is recorded for us in Mishnah Rosh Hashanah. Witnesses would look expectantly for the new moon on the expected days. When the moon was seen, the witnesses would go to the Sanhedrin and testify of what they had seen. The Sanhedrin would then declare the beginning of the month. This process seems simple enough.

The problem with this is that we don't know what Jesus was honoring when He kept the calendar in the first century. Did He keep the calendar in this way because seeing the sliver of the moon in the sky is the proper way to declare a new month, or did He keep it this way because the elders of the community had the authority to declare the beginning of the month? In the first century these were one and the same. There was no divergence.

Unfortunately, there is a divergence today. The Hillel II calendar over the many centuries of faithful witness has reached the point where it no longer aligns with the sighting of the sliver of the new moon by a day or more most years. This leaves the modern worshiper with a conundrum. Do we observe the calendar according to the sighting of the moon, or do we keep the calendar according to perceived authority of the Hillel II Calendar? Which is the weightier matter in this instance?

Even something so simple as what day to celebrate is now impossible to determine with any confidence. That is not to say that those who choose one interpretation over the other don't do so with confidence, rather that the confidence that they exhibit is in their own interpretation of Jesus' actions, and not any reflection of absolute truth.

So does this mean that we should not engage in a Passover memorial celebration? After all, we cannot truly observe Passover as written. I pray that this book lays to rest any thoughts along those lines. While the Passover Seder may only be a memorial of a memorial, it is packed full of profound meaning. Whether you get the day correct or not should not be a cause of worry. Whether you eat lamb or goat or chicken is not an important matter. Whether you celebrate on the 14th according to Hillel or some sighting of the moon, or on the Sunday following is not the issue.

What is important when it comes to celebrating Passover is that you get together with your local community of fellow believers and memorialize this important event in the lives of all who have been redeemed. Sure, you can keep it at home with your family. I certainly did it this way for my first experience. But Passover is not meant to be memorialized in isolation from others. The whole point of Passover is to share stories of redemption. The story begins in Egypt 3500 years ago and continues through the death of Jesus and into our own lives. Share a meal with other believers full of praise and testimony. Recount publicly what God did for Israel in Egypt and what He has done for you. We have all been there. We have all been saved out of slavery to sin and death and we have all passed through the waters of death. Passover now serves as a way to come together as a family and share the testimony of that event.

The Seder: A How To Guide

One of the first questions that arises when deciding to observe Passover, particularly for those who are new to the meal, is how to go about it. Just as with my first Passover, everything can seem foreign and awkward. The traditional ceremony with its script, songs, call and response, and communal readings can be daunting. This is natural. Understand that God does not expect any certain way of memorializing the event. No one is going to be condemned for doing things wrong when it comes to Passover. Simply gathering together over a meal and sharing stories of what God has done in the world and in your life is enough. Doing this will bring glory and honor to God and will serve as a memorial, a reminder, of what He has done for us. If this is all you want for your Passover, then you can begin to plan now without continuing any further. If, however, you would like to have a guide to a more formalized Seder, then continue reading.

The Passover Seder is a beautiful event. The elements of the Seder, while many may have originated in Roman banquet practices, have each become meaningful symbols in their own right. Each element describes an aspect of the first Passover and our own personal experience of Passover Redemption. So let's go through each of the elements and each of the major movements of the ceremony and provide some insight.

The Haggadah

When partaking in a Passover Seder, the first item that you will need is a Haggadah. The Haggadah is an order of ceremonies so to speak, and provides the script for the evening. The word Haggadah simply means "The Telling," and it will guide you through the ceremony. At a minimum, the Master of the ceremony should have a haggadah, but with responsive readings, the ceremony is much easier if each participant has their own copy.

There are many Haggadahs that are available. These range from the strictly Jewish Haggadah that contains many Rabbinic stories and traditions to the fully Messianic Haggadah that has little to nothing in common with the traditional Jewish ceremony. This book contains a companion Haggadah that is based on the traditional Jewish experience, but which I have modified to make clear the Christian fulfillment and foundation of Passover.

This Haggadah or any other can be used to lead a Passover Seder. Before the meal, the leader of the ceremony should read through the Haggadah aloud at least once to familiarize himself with what is expected of him.

Once you are ready for the ceremony, it is time to gather together the various elements of the Seder that will be needed for the meal.

The Elements

The Seder contains many elements that will require some logistical planning to be done before holding the Seder. Some of these elements will be on a specific plate while others should be accessible by all participants throughout the Seder. The ceremony itself is also broken up into sections that describe the events and the path of redemption. The elements and the ceremony work together to bring the Passover Seder to life.

Seder Plate

The first item that will be needed is a Seder plate for each participant in the Seder, or for each table, depending on how the Seder is going to be run. This plate can be anything from a traditional seder plate with six cups in it which will hold each of the food items that are part of the Seder ceremony, to a simple plate or platter on which the elements have been separated from each other.

If your seder plate is one that will be shared by multiple people, be sure that the various bowls are large enough to accommodate the number of people that will be sharing from each plate.

Maror and Chazeret - Bitter Herbs

One of the main features of any Seder is the maror, or "bitter herbs." This particular element is the only item on the Seder plate that is specifically commanded to be eaten in scripture. The bitter herbs are meant to be a reminder of the suffering that Israel experienced while in slavery to Egypt, but it also represents the bitterness that we experienced when in slavery to sin and death.

When the time in the ceremony comes to eat the bitter herbs, each participant is to eat enough bitter herbs to bring a tear to their eyes. It is supposed to hurt. For this reason, horseradish is commonly used. Other options for maror include lettuce (Chazeret), endives, onion, or dandelion. Pro tip, if you get horseradish, make sure that it is not a horseradish sauce. These condiments have the flavor of horse-radish, but have had all of the heat removed through the addition of other items. If you truly want a mind-blowing experience, eat the horseradish root straight up, or grind it and add some vinegar about a week before your Seder.

Because the word for bitter herbs is found in the plural in scrip-ture, there are two places on the Seder plate for the Maror. Typically when the ceremony gets to this point, both chosen options for maror will be eaten together. For example, if you use horseradish and lettuce as I do, then simply wrap the horseradish in a leaf of lettuce and dig in! Don't hold back. Remember, this is supposed to hurt enough to bring a tear to your eyes.

The remaining items of the Seder plate are purely traditional and can be included or discarded at the desire of the Seder planners.

Zeroa - Shankbone

In a traditional seder you will find on your plate a single bone. The word Zeroa literally means "arm" as in God saved Israel with an outstretched arm. This bone or slice of bone is not meant to be eaten, and it is not mentioned in the ceremony. Rather, it is purely symbolic. There are many options available. Some Judaica outlets sell slices of the bones of lambs to be used for this purpose. Other traditional options are a neck bone or wing bone of a chicken. This bone should be roasted and completely dry before placing it on the plate.

The zeroa bone is meant to act as a reminder of the Passover Sacrifice. The sacrifice which protected Israel from the outpouring of judgment on Egypt. Because the Seder does not include a sacrifice of any sort, this bone points to this fact. Thus the bone is not handled throughout the ceremony, rather it simply sits in its place untouched. A continual visual cue that the entire ceremony and meal is only a memorial of what is described in the Bible.

Beitzah - Hard Boiled Egg

A traditional Seder plate will also feature a hard boiled egg. Unfortunately there is no consensus as to when the egg originated on the plate, or what it is meant to symbolize. Beitza is the name of a tractate in the Mishnah that deals with holiday sacrifices, and so for many, this egg is representative of the special sacrifices (Numbers 28-29) that were meant to be part of the temple service for each of the Hebrew Festivals.

Other sources state that the egg is supposed to be representative of the cycle of life, death, and rebirth that is one of the tri-themes of

Passover as discussed in part one of this book. These sources also point to the time of the year in which Passover occurs. Spring is a time of life and rebirth, and so the claim is that the egg is included for this reason. This view connects the ideal of the egg of Passover plate with the eggs that are part of the Easter celebration as the symbolism is the same for both.

Finally, other sources state that the egg is a traditional symbol of mourning. In a hard-boiled egg, the potential life of the bird inside has been cut short and so the egg represents sadness. In this view, the egg is part of the Seder plate to represent a sense of mourning that should be part of Passover in recognition of the destruction of the temple. Once again, the traditional Seder plate has a reminder that Passover, and its accompanying sacrifices, cannot be kept as described in the Bible.

In the ceremony, the egg is not mentioned at all. It sits on the Seder plate and is removed just before the meal is brought to the table and is added to the meal. The participant eats the egg, often dipping it in salt water which, as will soon be seen, is often on the table as part of the ceremony.

Charoset

The word charoset is reserved for this particular dish as it is derived from the word cheres which means "clay." This item is a pasty substance that is made from apples, grapes, figs, dates, or pears, nuts, and wine with various spices. The first mention of Charoset is in the Mishnah in connection with unleavened bread and lettuce as part of the Passover meal.

Charoset is said to represent, in both texture and color, the mortar of the bricks that Israel made while slaving under Pharaoh. Again, this item is not mentioned in the haggadah as part of the Passover ceremony. Rather, as was shown earlier, this was likely a Roman dish that was incorporated into the Seder that is meant to act as an appetizer to the main meal. This is appropriate symbolically as it was before Passover that the mortar that this element symbolizes was used by Israel in Egypt.

Karpas - Greens

The final element on the Seder plate is the Karpas. Karpas simply means "Greens." Traditionally this is parsley, but can also be green onion or lettuce. In some parts of the world a potato is used. While the vegetable used is not symbolic of anything particular, it is what is done with this vegetable in the ceremony that gives it meaning.

Near the beginning of the ceremony everyone will take a piece of their karpas and will dip it twice in salt water. The karpas in this event serves simply as a delivery method for the salt water. The salt water on the other hand is said to be representative of the tears that were shed by Israel as they cried out to God for salvation under the burdens of Egypt. Again, the sorrow of life before redemption is a central part of the Seder experience.

With these items your Seder plate is complete, however, you do not need all of the items in order to hold a Seder. The bare minimum requires only the Maror. If you use the Haggadah that comes with this book, all you will absolutely need is the Maror (bitter herbs) and Karpas (Greens) and an accompanying bowl of salt water. Each of the other items can be included or discarded at the discretion of the Seder planners.

On the Table

There are other items that should be on the table to be used as part of the Passover Seder which will not be on the Seder plate. Again, some of these items are traditional and some are found in the commands associated with Passover. Most of these other items will be necessary if you are using the haggadah that accompanies this book.

Fruit of the Vine

One of the main features of the Passover Seder is four cups. Tradition states that this should be wine, but feel free to substitute grape juice as well. Each of these four cups has its own meaning that is explained at the beginning of the Seder ceremony.

The four cups represent aspects of our relationship to God and they create a path of redemption that is represented by the flow of the Seder in the other elements of the ceremony.

> Say therefore to the people of Israel, 'I am the LORD, and I will bring you out from under the burdens of the Egyptians, and I will deliver you from slavery to them, and I will redeem you with an outstretched arm and with great acts of judgment. I will take you to be my people, and I will be your God, and you shall know that I am the LORD your God, who has brought you out from under the burdens of the Egyptians.
> —Exodus 6:6-7

"I will bring you out from under the burdens of the Egyptians." The first cup is the cup of sanctification or separation. It symbolizes the removal of the believer from the presence of Egypt. No longer is the one who is brought out of Egypt part of Egypt. Now, because of what God has done on our behalf we are separated from Egypt.

"I will deliver you from slavery to them." The second cup is the Cup of Blessing. In Exodus 6, the second thing that God promises for

Israel is to deliver them from slavery. This act of being brought out of slavery is a blessing to all who have experienced it, and so we drink from this cup.

"I will redeem you with an outstretched arm and with great acts of judgment." The third cup is the cup of redemption through judgment. God promises to redeem Israel with an outstretched arm and mighty acts of judgment. The cup symbolizes redemption for Israel and for those who drink from it, as well as judgment through destruction for those who do not drink or who drink unworthily.

It is at this point in the companion haggadah that a time of communion is held. This cup is one that it is recommended that anyone who is present at the Seder who is not a believer in Jesus as Messiah not drink. As Paul says in 1 Corinthians 11, any who drinks the cup of communion in an unworthy manner is guilty of sin and subject to judgment. This introduction and reminder is part of the companion haggadah as the command for communion is a central part of the events of Passover.

"I will take you to be my people, and I will be your God." The final cup is the cup of Acceptance. This cup is based on the promise that God will take us to be His people and He will be our God. The final step of a relationship with Him.

These four cups serve as stepping stones of sorts as the Seder progresses. Each of the cups represents an   aspect of the Passover experience as the worshiper celebrates the process from separation to blessing to redemption and finally to acceptance. The seder steps through each of these and the cups serve as signals of transition from one topic to the next.

When you set your Passover table, be sure that you have enough drink for four cups for each participant. If you choose to use wine, also get some grape juice for children and anyone who does not wish to drink alcohol. It is also a good idea to think through how the various cups are to be filled during the ceremony. Are there appointed servers that are to fill the cups throughout the event, or are the pouring vessels to be passed around the table and each person is responsible for filling their own cups? Each method has its own benefits and drawbacks so be sure to address this during the planning phase.

It is also good to recognize that four cups of wine will cause some tipsiness in even the most seasoned of drinkers. Plan accordingly for how to proceed after the Seder event to allow for enough time for drivers to sober up. This can mean providing places to sleep, using this night as an all night vigil. A "night of watches," as is described in Exodus 12:42. This can also be done by cutting off all alcohol as soon as the Seder is complete and creating a time of fellowship, praise and worship, or testimony. Or finally having designated drivers to drive participants home after the event. Use your imagination and don't be afraid to prevent participants who have imbibed from leaving before having an opportunity to allow the effects of the alcohol to pass.

Matza - Unleavened Bread

No Seder is complete without unleavened bread. This element is essential for the Seder as nearly every Haggadah will make use of it in some manner, and the Passover Seder will technically occur on the first day of the Festival of Matzah. The matza used for this can be homemade or store bought. Be aware that store bought matzah will have the consistency of a cracker. Homemade matzah can range from crisp to a softer consistency similar to pita bread.

When it comes to matzah for Passover there may be some confusion. There are types of matzah in stores that state on the box that it is or is not suitable for Passover. This simply indicates whether the flour that was used for the matza was observed by Rabbinic authority to have been treated in a way that would prevent it from encountering any moisture and was baked within a certain time limit after being mixed with any moisture. Judaism has created a whole industry to ensure that from field to oven some matzah has never had the chance to begin to leaven even the slightest bit.

Your tolerance for this is up to you. You may wish to be as precise as Rabbinic authority accomplishes, in which case you will want to look for matzah that has been certified for Passover. Otherwise any unleavened bread that you can buy or make will suffice for the experience.

When preparing the table, be sure to place one to three pieces of matzah at the place of the leader of the ceremony. Three for if the leader will be making the "Hillel sandwich" which is part of a traditional Seder, and one if the leader will not do this. The companion haggadah does not include the Hillel sandwich portion of the seder, so if using this haggadah use only one. These pieces of matzah are usually placed under the seder plate that is used by the leader.

The history of the Hillel sandwich tradition is founded in the desire of some ancient rabbis to ensure that they had fulfilled all of the commands of Passover and so they would place bitter herbs and the meat for the meal between two pieces of matzah and eat all three in one bite. As stated before, you can include or not as you see fit. Be aware that many haggadahs include this practice so check yours and make your decision before the event.

For the other participants, matzah can be placed under their plates as well, or you can stage communal plates of matzah on the table that participants can take from. There are two times in the companion haggadah, one before the meal and one after, when each participant will need access to matza.

For the Christian, the matzah symbolizes the body of Jesus. This should be obvious as the matzah is used during communion, but the symbolism goes deeper than that. Matzah generally has holes in it, and is obviously without leaven. These can be used to point to the sinless nature of our Messiah and the fact that He was pierced on Passover for our sins.

At one point in the Seder the leader will break one of the pieces of matzah under his plate. The smaller half will be eaten when the time comes to eat the matzah and the larger half is to be placed in a bag and hidden somewhere in the room by one of the adult participants. This is the afikomen. For Christians, this represents the broken body of the Messiah and the idea that the world only experienced a portion of His power during His first ministry. The greater part of His power is to be sought after and attained after the Passover of salvation in the life of the believer.

Salt Water

Another item that should be staged along the table is small bowls of salt water that can be accessed by all participants. This water should be completely saturated with salt so that some crystals remain floating in the bottom of the bowl. Near the beginning of the Seder all participants will be instructed to dip the karpas twice. After this, the salt water is not used as part of the ceremony again. For those who include an egg on the Seder plate, this water can be used for dipping the egg during the meal. As stated before, this salt water represents the sorrow and tears which Israel cried while in slavery in Egypt.

Washing Bowl

One of the first things that is accomplished in the Seder is a ritual washing of hands. This hand washing is not meant to actually get the hands clean, but is purely symbolic. It demonstrates the desire of the participant to enter into Passover with clean hands and a pure heart as spoken of in Psalm 24:4. When it comes to practically accomplishing this hand washing there are several ways that this can be done.

The first option is to have a hand washing bowl at each table. Then when the time comes the bowl can be passed, or the safer option, each participant can proceed around the table and dip their hands in the water. Another option which can be employed when there are several tables involved is to have a central bowl that everyone can file past as a hymn is sung. Finally, a faucet can be made available so that all participants can file past and wash their hands. The best option for this is a kitchen faucet, but a bathroom faucet can work in a pinch. Regardless of which method you choose, be sure to have towels on hand for participants to dry their hands on when they are finished.

Elijah's Cup

In a traditional seder, there is a place of honor that is set at the table at which no one sits at. This place can be simply held by a decorative cup, or can include an entire place setting. This cup is meant to be set for the prophet Elijah. In Judaism, the prophet Elijah is supposed to precede the Messiah to announce His coming. This tradition forms the basis of the questions that Jesus faces in the Gospels concerning the coming of Elijah. Because of this, a place is set for Elijah to fill when the time of the Messiah is near. In a traditional seder, a moment is taken near the beginning of the seder to open the door and invite Elijah to come in and dine with the rest of the participants.

This particular practice has been cut from the companion haggadah, because as Christians we know that Elijah has already come preparing the way for our Messiah and Savior Jesus (Matthew 17:10-13). Many Jews still engage in this practice, so if you attend a traditional

Jewish Seder, this is what is happening when the leader opens the door to the room in the middle of the Seder, and this is what the cup that sits alone symbolizes.

And that is it. With the table set and the plates arranged, the time has come for the ceremony to begin.

The Ceremony

The Passover ceremony is a beautiful journey that tracks the process of redemption as modeled in the events of the Exodus. The meal has four major movements with each movement being initiated with a cup of wine. What follows each cup is then connected to the theme of that cup. Not all events attached to Passover are limited to the seder memorial meal however. There are rituals and ceremonies that can occur in the week preceding the Seder or after. As this book draws to a close, let's not focus on the Seder itself. Rather, let's step back and get a larger glimpse of a series of events that can accompany the celebration of Passover for a Christian.

Foot Washing

One of the first things that can be attached to the celebration of Passover is a foot washing ceremony. In John 13, after the Last Supper, Jesus washes the feet of His disciples. While doing this He says something important:

> If I then, your Lord and Teacher, have washed your feet, you
> also ought to wash one another's feet.
> —John 13:14

In the first century, most people wore sandals as their footwear. Open toes and heels with a strap on top to hold a strap of hardened leather to the bottom of the feet. The first century also featured a distinct lack of cars, trucks, or other vehicles for travel and transportation. Instead animals were used to accomplish these tasks. One fact that should be plainly obvious is that all vehicles have emissions and the emissions that accompany animals gather in the same place that feet go. This would leave a person with feet that would become rather disgusting in a short time.

Added to this, the feet of a person were seen as the most shameful part of the human body. We don't recognize this in our culture, but in a culture that was centered around matters of honor and shame, coming into contact with the foot of another person was an act of humiliation. Washing the feet of another was reserved for slaves. Only the lowest of the low touched the feet of another person. To do so demonstrated a position of shame and abject service. It is into this cultural context that Jesus, as Lord, Master, and Messiah, compels His own disciples to engage in foot washing with each other.

It is because of this verse that many denominations have taken the words of Jesus as a command that is to be carried out. On the Thursday of the week leading up to Pascha the Catholic, Eastern Orthodox, Anglican, and many Protestant denominations engage in a foot washing ceremony as part of the week's festivities. Holding a foot washing ceremony is a great way to engage in an act of service towards fellow believers.

The words of Jesus in John 13 are impactful, but there are many who understand this command of Jesus to be a command of principle and not specific action. In this view, it is an attitude of service to others that is being commanded here, and is not limited to the washing of feet. These words in John 13:14 are seen as connected to John 13:34 and the new command that Jesus gives to His disciples. This new command is that the disciples love one another as Jesus has loved them which was demonstrated through the command of foot washing and all of the cultural assumptions that went along with this practice. In this view we find a connection to what the Midrash has to say about the shamash, the servant, being the hero of the Passover feast.

Whether or not you hold a foot washing ceremony as part of your Passover celebration is up to you. This ceremony can occur just before the Seder or at any other part of the week leading up to Passover. If you do choose to incorporate foot washing into your memorial, here are a few tips to help you successfully incorporate this practice into your celebration.

Make sure that you have pitchers for carrying the water and basins that fit both feet and water. When you fill the pitchers make sure that the water is not too cold and definitely not too hot. Use the inside of your wrist to test the water. Finally, make sure that everyone has a towel to dry off. It is a good idea to mention beforehand that this will be happening and that everyone should bring their own towels. When we host a Passover event we have everyone bring their own basins to ensure that there are enough to go around.

The first time that we attempted a foot washing as part of our Seder we had people fill their own basins and carry the basin to the place where they would have their feet washed. When filling their basin, my son and his friend made their water way too hot. When my son plunged his feet in the water without first testing the temperature, he kicked the basin over and the water spilled all over the floor. The next fifteen minutes were spent cleaning up the spill, and the somber and serious ceremony descended into chaos. Recapturing that attitude took some time.

The same goes for the hand washing part of the Seder. It is easy for a basin of water to be knocked over or spilled, so choose a means of accomplishing this that works best for your space and the people who will be attending.

The Four Cups

Another opportunity to spill and create chaos in the midst of the Seder when it comes to pouring the four cups. Deciding how to accomplish this can be one of the most important decisions of your seder for this reason. If you are holding a non-alcohol seder, then consider pouring the grape juice into a pitcher that will not spill. If wine, then bottles work.

This particular part of the ceremony will likely be the determining factor on whether you have designated servers who are tasked with filling the cups and bringing plates or dishes to the table, or whether you allow the participants to pour their own drinks and have a buffet style event. When the cups are drained at various points in the service, refilling will cause a commotion regardless of the method that is chosen. The leader should not be afraid to stop for a time to allow all of the cups to be refilled before resuming.

Another point to consider, especially when offering wine, is if you allow the participants to pour their own. Be aware that there will invariably be some who will pour more than four cups of wine during the evening. This can potentially lead to all sorts of undesirable behavior and only increases the need to address the question of how the participants will get home if needed.

The Four Questions

At one point in the ceremony there will be four questions asked. The tradition with these four questions is to have the youngest participant either read or recite these questions. Among the questions is one that is "On all other nights we eat either sitting up or reclining;

why on this night do we all recline?" The glaringly obvious disconnect that will be apparent in most Passover celebrations is that modern participants will not be reclining at all. The companion haggadah retains this question for the sake of tradition. Don't feel as if you must recline for the sake of the question. This question does not need to be taken literally, but rather is intended to emphasize the fact that we can rest and relax because we have personally experienced a Passover event and therefore do not need to be physically prepared to leave as those participating in the first Passover were required to be. We can relax and recline and take our time in the memorial.

Midrash on Deuteronomy 26

In Deuteronomy 26, we read about the ritual that an Israelite was to go through when bringing their first-fruits before God in the temple. In this passage there is a declaration that is to be made by the believer as the offering was being presented. Part of the traditional seder is to dig into this passage and plumb its depths, and so the haggadah offers a midrash on these verses.

The word Midrash is derived from the word "drash" which means to seek or enquire. The word midrash, then, means to study intently. Specifically, midrash speaks of a Jewish interpretive technique which requires the reader to incorporate verses from throughout the Bible into the specific text that is being studied. When you read a verse and a word of phrase occurs that reminds you of something else that has been said elsewhere in the Bible, then the other passage is included in the study in order to learn more about the original.

Thus, the companion haggadah contains a traditional midrash on the passage Deuteronomy 26:5-8. What does the declaration that accompanies the firstfruits tithe have to do with Passover? First of all, Passover was a time when firstfruits were to be brought to the temple as a form of tribute to a king. In this we find that many of the themes of Passover present themselves through the text of this passage. We are a nation because of what the LORD accomplished for us and He is our king. Secondly, much of the story of the Exodus is told in this declaration. From Aram to Canaan to Egypt. Israel remained a separate people while there. The Egyptians put Israel into bondage, and they cried out to God for deliverance and He delivered Israel out with an outstretched arm and mighty hand. This short declaration holds within it the entirety of the story of the Exodus, and it is this reason that was provided as the foundation for why Israel owed God their allegiance and tithes. The midrash of this passage dives into just why we, too, owe God everything.

The Psalms

In the Bible, Psalms 113 through 118 are known as the Hallel Psalms. The name that has been given to these psalms, hallel, is a Hebrew word that simply means praise, not to be confused with Rabbi Hillel II who is credited with creating the Jewish calendar. This is not the same Hillel who created the tradition of the Hillel Sandwich. These psalms are each psalms of extended praise. It is these songs that were sung by the people while waiting for the presentation of the Passover lamb. These are also psalms that were sung by those who were waiting in the court of gentiles as they waited to enter the outer courtyard to sacrifice. For those who kept Passover with a temple sacrifice in the first century, the recitation of these Psalms controlled the timing of entry into the outer courtyard according to the Mishnah. It is from this mention that scholars have been provided a starting point when they attempt to determine how many temple sacrifices could have occurred in the first century.

These Psalms were central to the temple at all times and Passover specifically. In these Psalms we find references to the Exodus from Egypt, the splitting of the Red Sea, the giving of the Torah, the resurrection of the dead, and the pangs of the Messiah. All of these are poignant reminders of what God has done, and point to what God still intends to do in our world.

In the companion haggadah, all of the hallel psalms are read aloud but are split into two phases. Psalm 113 and 114 are read before the meal. One recited by the leader alone and the other recited by all participants. The second part of the Hallel recited after dinner and after communion. This time, only recited by the leader. Then followed by a call and response reading of Psalm 136.

In Psalm 136 the leader should take a moment to explain that the response phrase, Ki LeOlam Chasdo and its meaning and pronunciation. This passage is often translated as "His mercy endures forever." The word chasdo in this verse is the word chesed that was discussed in part one. Please take a moment to familiarize yourself with what this word means, and feel free to explain this depth of meaning to the participants of the Seder. You may decide to simply have the participants respond in English, Hebrew, or some other language at this point. If Hebrew, you will also need to take a moment to pronounce the phrase for the participants. This phrase is pronounced like it is spelled for the most part. kee lay o-LAHM choz-DOE. The one thing that will be different between how it is spelled in English and how it is pronounced in Hebrew is that the ch in chasdo is not the ch sound that English speakers are familiar with. Instead it is closer to the English H but with the H pronounced from the back of the throat when done properly. This can create a sound that may sound a bit like clearing your throat which is not easy for English speakers to accomplish and may require some practice. Feel free to choose whatever language will speak best to the participants at your Seder. Also, feel free to replace mercy with "covenant loyalty," from the earlier discussion on chesed.

Diyenu

Another mainstay of the Passover seder is the singing of a Hebrew song that is named Diyenu. For most of us in the west, we will not be able to sing this song as we do not know the words in Hebrew and the English translation does not fit the tune. Regardless, the chorus is quite easy to learn as the only word is Diyenu.

This word Diyenu is important as it encompasses the idea of "It would have been enough." This song is then a progression of things that God did for Israel while leading them out of Egypt and after each moment, the declaration is made that "It would have been enough." We would be content and owed God our allegiance for any one of the things on this list. If He had only done this one thing and no more, it would have been enough, but because of His grace, mercy, and compassion, He gave abundantly on our behalf.

Communion

Like foot washing, the sacrament of communion was commanded at the Last Supper. Unlike foot washing, communion is a command that no one debates regarding whether or not it should be kept physically. Part of the reason for this is that communion is spoken of later in the Epistles by Paul in several places in the letters to the Corinthians.

What is up for debate among believers is whether this practice is something that should be done at any time, as often as weekly, or only at Passover, as often as yearly. I am not going to dip my toes into this debate. Whether you believe that Communion is a weekly observance or yearly, the Passover Seder is an appropriate time to engage in this ancient ritual.

The companion haggadah has communion as part of the ceremony, and in this haggadah it is directly connected to the third cup,
the cup of redemption and judgment. During this part of the ceremony there is a moment of silence to allow the participants to do
an internal inventory of any remaining spiritual leaven that needs to
be repented of and discarded. When you get to this point, do not be
afraid to let this time of silence go on for several minutes to accommodate those who need to make last minute confessions and repentance.
Don't feel like you need to rush through this time. Allow the Holy
Spirit to work in the hearts of all who are present.

Next Year in Jerusalem

At the close of the seder is a declaration of the desire of the Jewish
people from the time of the Bar Kokhba rebellion in 135 CE. When
Israel was scattered and Jerusalem was made off limits to Jews. Since
this time the desire of the Jewish people to return to Jerusalem became
overwhelming. The primary reason for this desire to return to Jerusalem is because this return was seen by post-exile Rabbis as a sign of the
return of the Messiah. Because of this, a final declaration was added
to the seder of this wish and desire for a return to Jerusalem. The exile
from Jerusalem was seen by Jews to have occured because of a failing
in righteousness on their part and so the whole Passover Seder became
another way to foster righteousness in Jewish populations. Regardless
of whatever else they might get wrong in their worship, at least they
were doing Passover as best as they knew how.

For Christians we can join together in unity and express our own
desire for the return of the Messiah and the restoration of all things by
lifting our voices in union with Jews and Christians from around the
world. We too desire the return of the Messiah and the institution of

the Messianic kingdom that will reign from Jerusalem. Because of our hope we lift our voices and declare our wish. Next year in Jerusalem.

Passover and You

The Passover Seder is an event unlike any other. This meal, and the ceremony that surrounds it, gives every believer the opportunity to act out the plan of God's redemption in our lives. It provides an experience that serves as a way to physically memorialize our own salvation and make it real year after year. Passover is an event that is an integral part of the life of every believer, and as such, it is an event that should be memorialized with all sincerity. We should all aim to remember this day and season in action so that we do not allow the truth of our salvation to grow cold.

This is the true power of Passover when you get down to it. Passover and all of its liturgy help to keep our minds focused on what God has done for us as a perpetual reminder that is more than mental. When approached properly, Passover becomes a time of renewal for our relationship with God. While clearing our homes of leaven, we are called to examine our lives for things that are not of Him—to discard those things that are contrary to God and to recapture the newness of our walk with Him. The Seder reminds us that we are obliged to tell the story of what God has done for us as we recount what God did for Israel so long ago. Taking two days off of work reminds us that our salvation has nothing to do with what we have accomplished. Perhaps most of all, Passover gives us the opportunity to do all of this together as a community. We gather together and share a meal with others who have also experienced Passover in their lives. Together we are unified as the redeemed Israel who is fully dependent on God's salvation. In this celebration, grand Biblical themes such as the war for creation, our own relationship with God, and our reasonable response to Him come alive in our midst. As we engage with the day and all that surrounds it, we find that the history memorialized by this festival informs our present as well as points to the future that is our hope.

Passover is an event that transcends space and time. It permeates the hearts of all who sincerely engage, and separates the people of God from the surrounding culture. On the flip side, Passover serves as a unifier. It brings together all who worship the God of Israel under the banner of God. Passover is more than a simple ritual. It has a very deep and real meaning to vast swaths of the population. It is something that is relatable to everyone who has been saved by the blood of the Lamb and who has passed through the waters of death.

Passover was introduced to a people who lived in slavery to an earthly tyrant. It was expanded to every human who suffers under the great spiritual tyrant. It marks the moment of release and freedom from forces of evil. Without Passover and the lamb that was slain on that day, the destroyer would have the right to consume all flesh. In Passover we find hope. Hope of a life lived in freedom. Hope of the great enemy of mankind defeated. Hope of living life in covenant with the God of creation. Hope of living life eternally in His presence.

There truly is a power to Passover that cannot fully be captured in word, or even in the memorial celebration. We try to catch it but are unable despite our best attempts. The reality of Passover and the truth that was demonstrated by our Messiah on this day surpasses everything. Passover is an event of sublime transcendence as past present and future, individual, community, and divine all collide together in one yearly celebration. Passover is a blessing to all who partake of the bread and the cup in remembrance of what our Messiah did on our behalf. If you have never participated in Passover, my prayer for you is that you will consider finding others who do or host your own. If you are celebrating Passover this year, whether this is your first or your

60th memorial of this day, I pray that because of this book, Passover in all of its facets will come alive for you like never before.

Shalom.

ABOUT THE AUTHOR
AARON BISHOP

Aaron Bishop lives in Greenville, SC with his wife, Rebekah, and two children. He is the lead teacher at Grafted Together fellowship and operates an online teaching and local outreach ministry called Darash Chai (Seek Life). You can find many of his teachings at www. seeklifesc.com.

Aaron is also the project leader on the Patterns of Life Bible, a project that seeks to explore the literary patterns of the Bible and make them accessible to laymen. To learn more about this project, go to www.patternsoflifebible.com.

The Power of Passover is Aaron's first book, and at the time of publication he is diligently working on his second.

Made in the USA
Middletown, DE
31 March 2023

27299552R00146